DESIGN STRATEGIES IN ARCHITECTURE

Napier University
Information S

DESIGN STRATEGIES IN ARCHITECTURE

an approach to the analysis of form

Geoffrey H. Baker
School of Architecture,
Tulane University, New Orleans

second edition

VAN NOSTRAND REINHOLD

I⒯P™ A Division of International Thomson Publishing Inc.

New York • Albany • Bonn • Boston • Detroit • London • Madrid • Melbourne
Mexico City • Paris • San Francisco • Singapore • Tokyo • Toronto

E & FN SPON
An Imprint of Chapman & Hall

London · Weinheim · New York · Tokyo · Melbourne · Madras

To Kieran, for all your encouragement and enthusiasm

Published by E & FN Spon, an imprint of Chapman & Hall, 2–6 Boundary
Row, London SE1 8HN, UK

Chapman & Hall, 2–6 Boundary Row, London SE1 8HN, UK

Chapman & Hall GmbH, Pappelallee 3, 69469 Weinheim, Germany

Chapman & Hall USA, 115 Fifth Avenue, New York, NY 10003, USA

Chapman & Hall Japan, ITP-Japan, Kyowa Building, 3F, 2-2-1 Hirakawacho,
Chiyoda-ku, Tokyo 102, Japan

Chapman & Hall Australia, 102 Dodds Street, South Melbourne,
Victoria 3205, Australia

Chapman & Hall India, R. Seshadri, 32 Second Main Road, CIT East, Madras
600 035, India

Distributed in the USA and Canada by Van Nostrand Reinhold,
115 Fifth Avenue, New York, NY 10003, USA

First published in 1989 by Van Nostrand Reinhold (International) Co. Ltd

Reprinted 1991,1993
Second edition 1996

© 1989 E & FN Spon
© 1996 Geoffrey Baker

Printed in Great Britain by St Edmundsbury Press Ltd,
Bury St Edmunds, Suffolk.

ISBN 0 419 16130 9 (E & FN Spon)

CONTENTS

ACKNOWLEDGEMENTS

This book draws together a selection of analytical material produced over two decades by myself and by students under my direction. I must give special mention to Simon Buckley, whose perceptive analyses of Warkworth, Siena and Assisi[1] have formed the basis of these studies in part two.

I am also indebted to Jeremy Blake, who has made an important contribution to the analysis of the Town Hall at Säynätsalo, and to students of the School of Architecture at the University of Arkansas who produced useful analytical work during my period of teaching at Fayetteville. All these studies have informed my research.

I must also thank Gordon Brooks for his coordination of the computer modelling which helped me to draw the diagrams of Richard Meier's Atheneum, and Beth Ledford and Chad Edby who generated the computer images.[2]

Although their work is not discussed in this book, and analyses of their buildings were done without consultation, I must thank Peter Ahrends, Richard Burton and Paul Koralek for invaluable feedback which has influenced the development of the analytical methodology.

Thanks are due to Ellen Weiss for help with the manuscript, and Margaret Hudson, Christine Hilker and Jean Middleton, librarians at the Universities of Newcastle-upon-Tyne, the University of Arkansas and Brighton Polytechnic, for all their help.

[1] 'Symbolism, situation and architecture: Shifting emphases in making places' Dissertation by Simon Buckley at the University of Newcastle-upon-Tyne, 1971.

[2] Atheneum : Analysis of Form, video, written and presented by Geoffrey Baker and produced by Gordon Brooks at the University of Arkansas, 1988.

PREFACE TO THE SECOND EDITION

As those who study and practice it will know, architecture is a complex and wide-ranging discipline. In this introductory reader, one of my tasks has been to select, from a myriad of issues, those that will hopefully prove most enlightening to those seeking to fathom its mysteries.

In a book such as this, brevity is important, the summary is necessary, and visual information has a special role. 'Headlining' and the double page spread are each intended to help effective communication, bearing in mind the purpose of the book and its readership.

In this second edition I have added a section that outlines the relationship between some current perceptions of science, art and philosophy, and how these impinge on architecture. As throughout the book, vast areas of knowledge have been distilled to form very short summaries.

I am well aware of my inability to do justice to such profundities by such an abbreviated approach, but as my purpose generally is to introduce subject areas, I hope some doors will have been opened that will tempt the reader beyond.

Geoffrey H. Baker, New Orleans, April 1996.

FOREWORD

I was surprised and delighted when Geoffrey Baker's analysis of our design for the National Gallery extension appeared in Architectural Design (January and February editions, 1987), and I am pleased he has included it in this publication.

I felt he had 'understood' most of the formal design moves we made in evolving the scheme — indeed he interpreted several design subtleties which I only felt intuitively, and until his exposition had not fully perceived. It seems he is able to clarify and describe a work of Modern Architecture in ways that others such as Wittkower have been able to do for historic buildings.

Surely his method and skill in explaining the design intentions which lead to the appearance of a new building is of more value to the public than the gratuitous jottings of the architectural journalists, who seem always (in the U.K.) to be writing from predetermined and irrelevant viewpoints. An exception (in the U.S.) is Ada Louise Huxtable who is able to visit a building without dragging behind her a sackful of prejudices.

Dr. Baker's article on the National Gallery project was like a breeze of fresh air, and I believe his ability to analyze and explain an architect's formal ambitions en route to a building form should be a basic credential and a responsibility for architectural writers, and should form a foundation for their criticism.

So I hope that Dr. Baker's skill will be appreciated by a new generation of architectural critics, that they will have a deeper and more sophisticated understanding of the design process related to a particular building, and that they will be able to communicate this to the intelligent reader who is surely striving to understand Modern Architecture.

For architectural students this publication is, of course, essential study matter.

James Stirling.

Salzburg : view of the city and castle

Unlike painting music or literature, architecture is of the earth. It belongs to the ground as a container for the activities of man and as such is part of his very existence. This intrinsic link is evident in the basic need for shelter — buildings give shelter and in so doing engage architecture in man's survival against the hostile forces of nature.

Architecture therefore becomes involved in emotional and practical needs that are quite different to the needs that are met by technology. A car, a radio, a TV, are not necessary in the way that buildings are, so architecture has a different role and can represent significant areas of life. Although concerned with space, form and the satisfaction of functional demands, arguably architecture's primary role is symbolic. Alone among the arts it can express the idea of government, the church or the monarchy — it can also symbolize home.

So architecture is quite distinct from the other arts, which can all be dispensed with. We can remove a painting, choose when to listen to music, leave a book on a shelf. Architecture is not like that because it creates not only the framework for personal or family life, it creates the framework for national life and thereby represents the prime characteristics of a culture.

A civilization can best be understood by its architecture because of the way buildings show the interests of a society, its organizational skills, affluence or poverty, the kind of climate and the attitude towards technology and the arts. In towns and cities the general structure of society can be understood through the medium of architecture, so it becomes the most pervasive mirror of man's presence.

Importantly, and again unlike the other arts, architecture exists in relation to two sets of conditions ; on the one hand buildings must respond to fundamental issues such as the need for shelter and for ideas to be symbolized, whilst on the other they must relate to a region, to a specific location, to topography, to the path of the sun, to variations of temperature, to the movement of people.

How then can architecture be understood? How can it be examined? To what, primarily does it respond? Broadly speaking, there are three key factors which affect architecture; buildings must respond to site conditions, functional requirements and to the culture in which they find themselves. Regarding the latter, the state of advancement of the culture will affect the kind of structure and materials used. To understand buildings, all three of these factors must be taken into account and this becomes possible by analysis.

In any analysis of architecture it is convenient to consider the various factors as forces, and to begin with, because buildings are set on the ground, the topography should be examined. Here the forces are clearly apparent — a river is a force, a road is a force, a hill is a force, trees are a force, the climate is a force — and there are many subtle gradings of these forces.

Similarly, taking the second key factor outlined above, in satisfying functional needs, the organization of a building may also be considered in terms of its force characteristics. Form may be either linear or centroidal, static or dynamic. A tower for example may be thought of as a dynamic vertical force or a bridge as a static horizontal force, a castle may be seen as a centroidal defensive force.

The third important factor which affects architecture is the force exerted by a culture. In Ancient Greece a particular culture evolved in relation to a special set of circumstances at a particular time. Attitudes developed in the areas of religion, philosophy, science, mathematics technology and art which led to an architecture which represented the main ideas of the culture.

Although we can understand the Greek civilization through the combined media of say art, philosophy and literature, architecture, by its special role draws these together so that they become embodied in buildings. The cultural forces are encapsulated in the architecture and it is not coincidental that this architecture and the cultural values which it represents have endured to the present day.

This crystalization of cultural forces in buildings has happened throughout history and in our own time the glass skyscraper represents vital features of the twentieth century, symbolizing our technological capacity and key concerns much as did the pyramids, the Greek temple or Gothic cathedral.

Athens : The Acropolis
A reconstruction according to G.P.Stevens

In the richness and experience of a lifetime, ideas and principles...
begin to be a source of freedom and power... now you are released
by way of glass and the cantilever and the sense of space which
becomes operative. Now you are related to the landscape... You
are as much a part of it as the trees, the flowers, the ground;
you can pick up the earth and the sky. You are now free
to become a natural feature of your environment and that, I
believe, was intended by your Maker. [1]

My prescription for a modern house: first a good site. Pick
one that has features making for character... then build your
house so that you may still look from where you stood
upon all that charmed you and lose nothing of what you
saw before the house was built, but see more.

Architectural association accentuates the character of the
landscape if the architecture is right. [2]

[1] Frank Lloyd Wright, a talk given to the Fellowship, quoted in Olgivanna
Lloyd Wright, Frank Lloyd Wright: His Life, His Work, His Words, Pitman,
1970, pp. 159-60
[2] Frank Lloyd Wright, In the Realm of Ideas Edited by Bruce Brooks
Pfeiffer and Gerald Nordland, Southern Illinois University Press,
Carbondale and Edwardsville, 1988, p 44.

PART ONE

PRINCIPLES OF ANALYSIS

THE ROLE OF ARCHITECTURE

1

FORCES

In his study of place, Genius Loci, Towards a Phenomenology of Architecture, Christian Norberg-Schulz explains the basic act of architecture as being 'to understand the vocation of the place.'[1] He describes the need 'to concretise the genius loci ... by means of buildings which gather the properties of the place and bring them close to man.'[2] Throughout the book Norberg-Schulz draws out those features of topography and landscape which give a special character to places and shows how architecture can respond by creating a meaningful environment.

In his discussion Norberg-Schulz constantly refers to man-made and natural forces as when he describes the siting of Prague as comprising 'all the main natural forces, undulating plain, rocky hills and water,'[3] explaining how the architecture in the city manages to embody this.

In the study, Norberg-Schulz first identifies the characteristics of the region, showing how the city became a nodal point where a road from Ucrania and Poland which crossed the Vitava into Germany met the road from Austria in the south to Saxony and Prussia. He describes how Prague is situated on an extended hill which rises at the curve of the river; the hill and the river being 'opposed but complimentary forces.'[4]

[1] C. Norberg-Schulz Genius Loci, Towards a Phenomenology of Architecture New York 1980 p. 23 [2] Ibid. p. 23 [3] Ibid. p. 99 [4] Ibid. p. 83.

Rome is seen as being at 'the centre of a landscape which contains everything,'[5] with the Piazza Navona demonstrating that the ideal equilibrium between nature and the culture has been achieved:

At Piazza Navona we are really 'inside', close to the earth, close to the palpable things of everyday existence, at the same time as we feel part of a comprehensive cultural totality. No wonder it has become the popular place of Rome par excellence. The synthesis of nature is condensed and visualized in Bernini's great fountain, where natural elements such as water and rocks are combined with human figures and religious symbols, as well as the axis mundi of the obelisk. In front of the church of S. Agnese, finally, we find another characteristic Roman element, a broad flight of stairs. In Rome, stairs are not used to create a distance between different existential realms; rather they represent the articulation of the ground itself. The great Roman stairs bring us close to the earth and increase our sense of belonging to the place.

Rome: Piazza Navona

[5] C. Norberg-Schulz, Genius Loci, Towards a Phenomenology of Architecture, New York, 1980. p. 164.

NATURE

In an essay discussing the relationship between art and nature, art and the world, John Berger argues that 'Nature is energy and struggle. It is what exists without any promise ... as an arena, a setting, it has to be thought of as one which lends itself as much to evil as to good. Its energy is fearsomely indifferent.'[1] He goes on to argue that we sense beauty because it is such a contrast to our struggle against nature.

> It is within this bleak natural context that beauty is encountered, and the encounter is by its nature sudden and unpredictable. The gale blows itself out ... Under the fallen boulder of an avalanche a flower grows ... beauty is always an exception, always despite of.
> This is why it moves us.

Berger asserts that the kind of aesthetic emotion we feel before a man-made object derives from the emotion we feel before nature:

> All the languages of art have been developed as an attempt to transform the instantaneous into the permanent. Art supposes that beauty is not an exception — is not despite of — but is the basis for an order.
> Art is an organized response to what nature allows us to glimpse occasionally. Art sets out to transform the potential recognition into an increasing one.[2]

[1] John Berger. An article in The Guardian, December 30th, 1985, p. 9

6

In his discussion Berger relates his argument to a white wooden bird, hung by peasants in their kitchens in certain regions of Czechoslovakia, Russia and the Baltic countries. These birds somehow manage to act as 'mediators' between man and nature.

As Berger explains, their figurative form, that of a dove, makes a direct reference to the world of nature. Being located indoors (where birds are not usually found) renders the object symbolic. Then there is respect for the way the material, wood, has been fashioned. There is also unity and economy in the object, a richness resulting from its design. Finally there is wonder as to how the object is made. This sense of mystery, the fine craftsmanship, provoke an aesthetic 'emotion.' Thus does man 'transform' nature into a work of art.

In a discussion of the cave paintings in Spain and southern France, Dr. Jacob Bronowski suggests that these works by early man 'act as a kind of telescope tube of the imagination ; they direct the mind from what has been seen to what can be inferred or conjectured.' [1]

He explains how art and science are both human actions deriving from the ability to visualize the future, playing a vital part in cultural evolution, which he describes as 'a constant growing and widening of the human imagination'. [2]

[1] J. Bronowski, The Ascent of Man, London, 1943, p. 54.   [2] Ibid, p 56.

ART AS SYMBOL

The link between art and man's emotions has been pursued by Susanne K. Langer, who has given her own definition of art: 'Art is the creation of forms symbolic of human feeling.'[1] She explains the importance of the term 'creation' because it is the creative act that produces the work of art. Merely to produce something is not enough; to erect a house is a mechanical act which is not the same as creating a work of architecture.

Discussing the content of forms Langer argues that what matters is their import so that they become 'logically expressive or significant forms. They are symbols for the articulation of feeling and convey the elusive and yet familiar pattern of sentience.'[2] The symbolic element is of the greatest importance because Langer asserts that art is always a symbol. 'In an articulate symbol, the symbolic import permeates the whole structure, because every articulation of that structure is an articulation of the idea it conveys.'[3]

Langer insists that in order to create significant form with an appropriate symbolic content an intellectual dimension is necessary. 'Works of art are made of sensuous elements, but not all sensuous elements will do.'[4] They must be capable of assemblage in the right kind of combinations; as symbols, works of art must communicate directly and immediately. 'An articulate form must be clearly given and understood before it can convey any import,' and 'the congruence of the symbolic form and the form of some vital experience must be directly perceived by the force of the Gestalt alone. Hence the paramount importance of abstracting the form, banning all irrelevancies that might obscure its logic, and especially divesting it of its usual meanings so it may be open to new ones.'[5]

[1] S.K. Langer, Feeling and Form, A Theory of Art, London, 1953, p. 40 [2] Ibid., p 52 [3] Ibid., p 52 [4] Ibid., p.56 [5] Ibid., p 59.

Pagoda, Yasaka 1618

POETRY

This discussion of art may be compared to Norberg-Schulz's assertion that 'the fundamental function of art is to gather the contradictions and complexities of the life world.' Quoting Heidegger he goes on to explain how man must dwell on this earth 'poetically'. 'Only poetry in all its forms (also as in the art of living) makes human existence meaningful, and <u>meaning</u> is the fundamental human need.' [1]

To Christian Norberg-Schulz 'architecture belongs to poetry' [2] and attains a poetic dimension when 'buildings gather the properties of the place and bring them close to man.' [3] As such architecture is also art, responding, as Berger insists, to man's desire to prolong the instantaneous into the permanent and to create order out of the chaos of nature.

It was in Ancient Greece, where the landscape is such that it became possible to identify the different characteristics of places, that man personified particular places as gods. Open air altars were formed so that man could contemplate a sacred landscape. Temples later gave form to this by extending the personification of the gods into an appropriate symbolic dimension.

Doric order column and entablature The Thesion Athens. 449-444 B.C.

[1] Norberg-Schulz *Op. Cit.*, p. 23. [2] Ibid, p. 23. [3] Ibid, p. 23.

The Parthenon crystallizes the cultural intentions of the Greeks by its siting, its presence, its precision and order. The frieze and pediments portray important aspects of Greek life.

As an art work the Parthenon demonstrates Berger's mystery and permanence, realising Norberg-Schulz's 'vocation' of place whilst also manifesting Heidegger's poetic dimension. Like the Egyptian pyramid and Gothic cathedral it gives meaning through form to a central idea shared by a culture.

The Parthenon Athens 449-444 B.C. architects Ictinus and Callicrates

Through its dedication to gods and goddesses, personified in human form, Greek architecture embraces human characteristics, with the masculinity of Doric and feminine associations with Ionic. Moreover, the Greek temple in its articulation presents a unified whole in which every part relates to a central idea, being linked to each other by a proportional system. The Greek temple therefore brings together man, nature and the gods in a comprehensive representation of the values of a culture.

MEANINGS IN USE

The Greek temple exemplifies the important distinction between a work of art for its own sake such as a painting or a piece of sculpture, and a work of architecture, which must serve a purpose.

Colin St. John Wilson quotes Alberti to emphasize that architecture 'is born of necessity'[1] and explains the unique nature of architecture as being that it is

> a special form of art — the transformation of utility into icon...
> It is, however, a condition of this transformation that its origins
> lie in use, are humble, always some need to shelter or enframe
> some action or object special to its culture, and that if it
> loses its roots in that necessity it loses its status as a
> transforming agent.[2]

Wilson insists that the meaning of architecture lies in use, and that buildings only come into being to serve the needs of a culture. He asserts that

> the limits of an architecture are the limits of the culture that it
> serves. It is the embodiment of values that have been worked out
> before by a culture in all its levels of awareness (religious, political,
> economic). The cathedral did not invent religion![3]

[1] L.B. Alberti : Ten Books on Architecture; bk 1 ch IX.
[2] Colin St John Wilson 'The Play of Use and the Use of Play' Architectural Review, July 1986, p. 14.   [3] Ibid. p. 18

Wilson points out that architecture must serve the needs of society in two ways, first

> to set up a spatial order that makes possible the fulfilment of manifold operations in an <u>effective way</u>. This is the base of common use.

> Second, to bring to life an order of representation that embodies those occasions so that they can be recognised in an <u>intelligible</u> way. [1]

If we consider either the great monuments of civilization or the humblest dwellings, we may relate them to Wilson's assertion that architecture "transforms utility to a level above that of necessity and thereby invents forms that truly celebrate a "way of life." " [2] He concludes this argument by quoting Wittgenstein's proclamation:

> Where there is nothing to glorify there can be no architecture [3]

ARCH OF TITUS ROME   A.D. 82

[1] St John Wilson, Op.Cit., p. 18   [2] Ibid., p. 18   [3] Ibid., p. 18 (taken from L. Wittgenstein, <u>Culture and Value</u>, p.69).

PRIMITIVE ARCHITECTURE

Banani a cliff debris-type village of the Dogon
Timbuktu Africa

Discussing the way house forms evolve, Amos Rapoport explains how in Primitive societies everyone is capable of building his own dwelling, with the average family having all the technical knowledge that is needed.[1]

This also means that the needs of the dwelling are understood perfectly with certain ways of doing or not doing things. Rapoport points out how

> Certain forms are taken for granted and strongly resist change, since societies like these tend to be very tradition oriented. This explains the close relationship between the forms and the culture in which they are embedded, and also the fact that some of these forms persist for very long periods of time.[2]

The Dogon live in a series of compact villages on ledges and rocky slopes at the foot of cliffs near Timbuktu. The villages are formed of houses and granaries, crops being stored in the granaries. Each man and woman has at least one personal granary. Houses and granaries are built by the men assisted by male members of his family and those of his neighbourhood.[3]

[1] Amos Rapoport, House form and culture, New Jersey, 1969. p. 3 [2] Ibid, p 4.

[3] For a full discussion of this see Aldo van Eyck's essays 'The Interior of Time' and 'A Miracle of Moderation'. Meaning In Architecture edited by Charles Jencks and George Baird, London 1969 pp. 171, 173.

14

VERNACULAR ARCHITECTURE

In Vernacular architecture the process of evolution using a model continues with adjustments and variations. The dwelling is now built by tradesmen. Vernacular architecture does not have theoretical or aesthetic pretensions and models develop in accordance with regional, climatic and economic factors.

Although in some ways limited, Vernacular models can be easily modified. This adaptability and the widely understood meanings inherent in such stereotypes ensures their authoritative role in society. In Britain and other derivative cultures the popularity and acceptance given to the neo-Georgian and neo-Tudor models indicate a strong preference for tradition. Such models have stood the test of time and are effective in both a practical and symbolic sense, far more so than the work of individual designers.

Rapoport explains the nature of folk architecture:

> The folk tradition... is the direct and unselfconscious translation into physical form of a culture, its needs and values—as well as the needs dreams and passions of a people... The folk tradition is more closely related to the culture of the majority and life as it is really lived than is the grand design tradition which represents the culture of the elite. [1]

Terrace housing in Brighton

[1] Rapoport Op. Cit., p. 2.

MONUMENTAL ARCHITECTURE

Funerary temple of Mentuhetep Dêr el Bahari 2065 B.C.

Historically, monumental architecture has given form to the collective ideals of a culture and has designated the hierarchical structure of society. Buildings such as the pyramid or temple acquired their symbolic role and conviction as a result of a long period of evolution.

This monumental architecture was concerned far more with its symbolic content than with utilitarian function, and in drawing upon greater resources and skills than ordinary buildings its course of development has been materially different.

The Egyptian Temple and Pyramids clearly demonstrate the principle which governs the development of monumental architecture. Such buildings tend to be wasteful in human resources, requiring a very considerable input of labour. They were built to impress rather than to inhabit and came into being as a result of the organizational skills that can only be supplied by a specialist, the designer or architect.

Because the role of monumental architecture has been primarily to communicate meanings of a very specific kind the forms are arranged in ways that give a high priority to aesthetic effects.

Whereas traditionally dwellings for the mass of the population assume meaning by fulfilling functional requirements related to protection and survival, it has been the function of monumental architecture to convey meanings concerned with ideals and status. Amos Rapoport has explained the phenomenon as :

> Monuments — buildings of the grand design tradition — are built to impress either the populace with the power of the patron, or the peer group of designers and cognoscenti with the cleverness of the designer and good taste of the patron. [1]

Villa Capra : Vicenza 1567 architect Andrea Palladio

Buildings such as the Villa Capra may be regarded as High Art. Such buildings demonstrate compositional principles based on theoretical propositions. A symmetrical arrangement ensures order, a system of proportional relationships ensures harmony, and the deployment of the classical language communicates meanings associated with elegance and enduring quality. There is a high degree of abstraction inherent in such works compared with the more practical concerns of the ordinary dwelling.

[1] Rapoport Op. Cit., p. 2.

CULTURE

In a discussion of the relationship between the individual and society, C. Norberg-Schulz explains how satisfactory cultural integration depends on the existence of common symbol-systems:

> From birth we try to orientate ourselves in the environment and establish a certain order. A common order is called culture. The development of culture is based on information and education and therefore depends on the existence of common symbol-systems. The culture integrates the single personality into an ordered world based on meaningful interactions. [1]

From the earliest times man has used language as his basic form of communication, a system whereby words have a meaning understood by all within an ordered grammatical framework. The inadequacy of words to express certain meanings has led to the development of non-verbal communication systems whose purpose is to assist and extend comprehension of aspects of experience. Science, the arts and music each extend our understanding of the world by means of constructions not possible within language alone, and architecture gives meaning to aspects of life that cannot adequately be conveyed by words.

[1] C. Norberg-Schulz 'Meaning in Architecture', Meaning in Architecture (edited by C Jencks and G. Baird) London, 1969. p. 220

Honington Hall Warwickshire England   c. 1685

Architecture has always played a leading role in the way an individual may be identified within a culture and certain styles evolved during the later middle ages which were concerned with status within the social hierarchy.

Status may depend on different things in the various strata of society but for the landowners and aristocracy of seventeenth century England it was important to demonstrate a subtle combination of wealth, power and good taste.

This need was met perfectly with the introduction of Italian Renaissance architecture into the country by Inigo Jones. The style was based on the work of Andrea Palladio in and near Vicenza, and the classical principles embodied in his villas were interpreted in a manner appropriate to the English landscape and climate.

Classical proportions, symmetry and the use of certain kinds of ornament and sculpture led to an architectural style whose meaning was shared by a social group. So effective was this particular symbol-system that it still pervades the English-speaking cultures as the neo-Georgian style.

PROGRAMME AND SITE

Sydney Opera House   1973 architect Jorn Utzon

In his seminal work, <u>Complexity and contradiction in architecture</u>, Robert Venturi explains that architecture occurs at the meeting of interior and exterior forces of use and space. This interaction is one of the basic generators of architectural form as demonstrated in Jorn Utzon's Sydney Opera House in which the particular function and location inspired an extravagantly picturesque solution. Two sets of forces determine the **concept**, those of the program and those of the site, using a constructional technology available to our twentieth century culture.

As Kevin Lynch has pointed out, it is necessary for man to locate himself in relation to his environment. He builds up a mental picture of recognizable features that mean 'home'.

A good environmental image gives its possessor a sense of emotional security.[1] He explains that it is by means of nodes, paths and districts that he can orientate himself... 'The world may be organised around a set of focal points or be broken into named regions or be linked by remembered routes.'[2]

IDENTITY   SPATIAL CONTEXT   MEANING

Lynch cites 'identity, the spatial context and meaning as the three components of an environmental image. He explains how a door has a clear identity in that it can be recognized as such, how it is part of a general space pattern which enables the observer to locate it in relation to everything else, and also has 'some meaning for the observer whether practical or emotional.'[3]

Florence Cathedral   1296 – 1462   architect   Arnolfo di Cambio.

To illustrate this on a completely different level, the cathedral at Florence has a clear identity, can easily be located in the street pattern and has unambiguous meaning as a religious centre.

[1] Kevin Lynch, The image of the city, Cambridge Mass. 1960 p. 4   [2] Ibid, p 7.   [3] Ibid. p. 8

MOVEMENT

The mobility of man has led to the creation of routes. These have their own energy and as such constitute forces.

As with differences in natural forces (a river is not the same as a stream) so too are there differences in the force characteristics of routes. A major highway differs from a suburban street, a railway has a particular kind of limited and concentrated movement potential.

Viaducts and bridges are similarly concentrated vectors of movement and as with all routes they establish a special kind of relationship with the landscape. Heidegger explains how bridges do not merely connect two banks but 'brings stream and bank and land into each others' neighbourhood. The bridge gathers the earth as landscape around the stream.' [1]

The Ziggurat of Urnammu Ur B.C. 2125

[1] Heidegger. Poetry, Language, Thought, New York. 1971. p. 152

Roman bridge across the Tagus, Alcantara Spain. A.D. 105-16.

Movement can be an important design generator and stairs, ramps, escalators and elevators also may be regarded as forces of different intensity.

As with Heidegger's bridge, each kind of movement has its own characteristics and a particular relationship potential with its immediate surroundings. Each of these devices has been fully explored architecturally at different periods in history, from the ramped approach to Babylonian Ziggurats to the twentieth century celebration of escalators and lifts.

The serene static quality of the arched Roman bridge in stone contrasts with the soaring drama of the lifts in the Hyatt Regency Hotel in Dallas. The vertical thrust is intensified by making the lifts visible and by juxtaposing their shafts so that they cut through the horizontal layers of balconies which look onto the atrium space.

This contemporary exploitation of movement as a significant design opportunity belongs to a tradition which includes such fine examples as the Scala Regia in the Vatican and Michelangelo's staircase to the Biblioteca Laurenziana in Florence.

Hyatt Regency Hotel Dallas Texas 1976-78 architects Welton Becket and associates.

VIEWS

Theatre Epidauros Greece c. 350 B.C.

If a route is a force resulting from man's mobility, a view also has force characteristics in terms of his ability to see.

Vincent Scully refers to the importance of views in the creation of special places in ancient Greece. He explains how Greek theatres were 'the primary device for attempting to bring city and landscape together' by pointing out how theatres at Megalopolis, Ephesus, Sikyon and the Piraeus in each case looked towards a distant view with conical hills.[1]

At Megalopolis all the holiest places of the city were laid out along the general axis of the view between the theatre and mountain cone. Scully reminds us that 'The importance of the theatre in creating sweeping views for Hellenistic cities can therefore not be overestimated.'[2]

He also mentions how some Hellenistic cities 'were like great theatres themselves, tipped forward on a height in order to achieve a dramatic view across the landscape.'[3] He describes how at Cassope the city is shaped like a theatre and how 'A mighty panorama opens out before it, while the savage mountains press up close behind its northern walls... the whole effect is of the city's command over an entire world of plain, mountains and the sea.'

[1] Vincent Scully, The Earth The Temple and the Gods, New Haven and London, 1962 (revised edition Yale University 1979) [2] Ibid., p. 194 [3] Ibid p 194.

STRUCTURE

Although structure may be seen as a means towards an end, structural devices in buildings can be an opportunity for expression. This was the case in the earliest civilizations and the Greek column became an expression of refinement which also was interpreted in different ways to have different meanings.

Similarly Roman and Romanesque architecture exploited the arch and vault in ways that were appropriately meaningful for their period. The use of the arch and vault enabled the Romans to span greater distances than the Greeks and Roman buildings exemplify the advanced technology of their culture.

The use of columns, arches and vaults in Romanesque architecture led to the soaring naves of the great cathedrals.

In the Gothic period the column became part of the vaulted system so that column and vault merge in a celebration of structural audacity and technical skills. The intention was to glorify God with a structural 'miracle' in which the heavy ground based characteristic of stone was transformed into apparent weightlessness.

St. Philibert Tournus France 950-1120
after Francis D. K. Ching.

Beauvais Cathedral original choir 1272
after a sketch by R. Branner

If structure can be thought of as conveying meaning it
may also be read as having force characteristics. These
relate to the way structure has to withstand such phenomena
as gravity, wind pressure, and soil characteristics.

The response, as in nature, produces geometrical solutions,
with rhythmic linkages to give strength and a sense of
elasticity or tension attributable to the way materials
are handled.

These characteristics are admirably described by John
Ruskin:

> Egyptian and Greek buildings stand, for the most
> part by their own weight and mass, one stone
> passively incumbent on another; but in the
> Gothic vaults and traceries there is a stiffness
> analogous to that of the bones of a limb, or
> fibres of a tree; an elastic tension and
> communication of force from part to part, and
> also a studious expression of this throughout
> every visible line of the building.

As D'Arcy Wentworth Thompson has explained [1] there are
limits to the size/strength ratio of materials and the
150' high Gothic choir vaults at Beauvais collapsed in
1284. No structure as tall was attempted again by the
medieval cathedral builders.

[1] D'Arcy Wentworth Thompson, <u>On Growth and Form</u>. Abridged edition edited by John
Tyler Bonner, Cambridge University Press, Cambridge, 1961 p.19.

27

STRUCTURE

Headquarters Building
HongKong and Shanghai Banking Corporation
Architects Norman Foster and Associates

In the twentieth century Le Corbusier saw the column as a symbol of freedom. Using a reinforced concrete slab supported by columns and beams, he could eliminate the need for closely spaced supports whether these be walls or columns.

This use of columns enabled great latitude with planning and using the term 'pilotis' Le Corbusier saw the column as a way of lifting buildings above the landscape to enjoy 'sun, space and greenery.'

More recently the High Tech. movement has used the expression of structure and service ducts to demonstrate not only a command of technology in building, but also the position of technology in the later twentieth century. Richard Rogers has exploited this in several buildings including the Pompidou Centre in Paris whilst Norman Foster's Headquarters of the HongKong and Shanghai Banking Corporation exemplifies the role of structure as an aesthetic device in a manner not dissimilar to that of the Gothic flying buttress.

Electronics Factory Swindon England 1965
Architects   Norman and Wendy Foster and Richard Rogers.

The tensile qualities of steel have enabled architects and engineers to provide often dramatic structural statements in which Ruskin's 'elastic tension' is clearly evident. Tubular steel, used in space frames or as support struts has given architects considerable flexibility in articulating the 'skin' of buildings

The external expression of structure induces a sense of dynamism and vitality widely accepted as characteristics of twentieth century life.

GEOMETRY

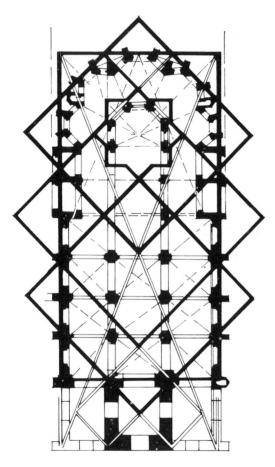

St. Peters, Riga.

Geometry is the organizing discipline of architecture. It is necessary for the arrangement of structure so that geometrical constructs are as inevitable as they are in nature. Geometry is also a means of relating all the parts of a building to one another.

Throughout history it has been realized that a proportional system can assist both the ordering and the perception of buildings. Mathematical proportional systems were used by the Greeks in their temples and they evolved a proportion relationship known as the Golden Section.

The Golden Section is based on a subdivision in which the lesser portion of a line is to the greater as the greater is to the whole or $\frac{x}{y} = \frac{y}{x+y}$. If a square be drawn within a Golden Section rectangle the remaining rectangle also has Golden Section proportions. The Golden Section was also used during the Renaissance and the medieval masons used a variety of sophisticated proportional systems to ensure harmonic relationships in churches and cathedrals.

GOLDEN SECTION RECTANGLE

Diamond Series Project House 8 1962-66
entry level plan and projection.
architect John Hejduk.

In the twentieth century Le Corbusier's geometric solutions
of the twenties have been emulated and extended by a
group of architects sometimes called The Five.[1] Of their
work Peter Eisenman's geometry is the most complex whilst
John Hejduk uses primary forms in powerful juxtapositions.

[1] Richard Meier, John Hejduk, Charles Gwathmey, Michael Graves
and Peter Eisenman. (The Five published a book illustrating
their work in 1972).

31

SUMMARY

FORCES

Natural phenomena and buildings can each be understood in terms of 'forces'. These differ in magnitude and intensity as with the difference between a mountain and a hill, a swift flowing river and a gently meandering stream. Architecture may be seen as an interaction between three sets of forces, those of the site, those of the program and those of the prevailing culture.

GENIUS LOCI

The term 'Genius Loci' refers to the spirit of places, those frequently elusive characteristics which make them unique. The finest examples of architecture capture this spirit and bring together qualities inherent in the landscape and the culture.

NATURE AND ART

John Berger argues that 'Art is an organised response to what nature allows us to glimpse occasionally. When Spring and Summer follow Winter we sense the contrast as beauty, our emotions are aroused. Art is therefore an attempt to make such transient aesthetic experiences permanent.'

POETRY

Poetry can be explained as an 'elevated expression of thought or feeling in metrical form.'[1] A poetic description differs from prose in that a subject is illuminated in ways that are imaginative and expressive. In architecture this poetic dimension transforms the ordinary into the significant so that as a container for living or working, the work of architecture may enrich life rather than merely sustain it.

[1] The Pocket Oxford Dictionary, Oxford, 1978. p. 682 (Edited by J.B. Sykes).

MEANING IN USE

Colin St. John Wilson insists that architecture must 'transform utility into icon.' It must serve a useful purpose within a culture and must be effective in so doing.

Buildings must not only demonstrate their purpose but must be intelligible, they must communicate their purpose clearly.

MATERIALS AND MEANING

The materials used in buildings have profound psychological implications. The extensive use of stone in various periods has increased the sense of monumentality in civic buildings and as a natural material stone also blends well into the landscape. Brick gives a more human scale to buildings and because of its cheapness and ease of manufacture has been used since Babylonian times for both domestic and public building. Brick is a friendly material unlike reinforced concrete which can appear hostile unless given a smooth finish. This hostility can be present in the use of steel and glass; mirror glass and sometimes tinted glass can create a sense of impenetrability which may be unsuitable for certain design tasks. Glass has become an important symbol in the twentieth century, matching the use of stone in previous civilizations. The failure of glass and steel to achieve a satisfactory rapport with users when forming office blocks or other public buildings has resulted in a shift back towards more solidity and a more 'friendly' surface treatment of many buildings.

Palazzo Pubblico Siena 1298

SUMMARY

PRIMITIVE ARCHITECTURE

In primitive societies everyone is capable of building his own house and certain forms evolve in response to people's needs, climate and available craft skills. These models become established and are resistant to change. The same form will be used for long periods of time partly because such forms embody meanings that are important to the society and are understood by everyone.

VERNACULAR ARCHITECTURE

In vernacular architecture, although the houses are built by tradesmen, models evolve which have shared meanings. These models respond to prevailing economic circumstances and also take account of regional climatic characteristics. Vernacular architecture is therefore an architecture of consensus, drawing together those issues of importance to society. In its twentieth century form, vernacular architecture takes account of the desire to conform, identification of social role, traditional associations and market forces.

Timber framed house Egerton Kent c. 1500.

Semi-detached houses Brighton England   1930s.

MONUMENTAL ARCHITECTURE

Unlike primitive and vernacular architecture, monumental architecture is built to impress and is largely concerned with aesthetic effects. Monumental architecture represents abstract theories and idealistic principles rather than practical issues but because of the need to communicate meanings shared by all, models evolve as they do in primitive and vernacular architecture. Such models as the Greek temple, the Medieval cathedral or Palladian country house emerge as much from a desire to communicate shared meanings as from a common technology. Monumental architecture may be regarded as High Art and may also be termed 'symphonic' in that it usually contains an elaborate composition of several contrasted but related parts.

CULTURE AND MEANING

For a culture to exist it is necessary for the individual to become integrated in 'an ordered world based on meaningful interactions'.[1] Non-verbal forms of communication are used to clarify certain intangible phenomena and architecture gives meaning to aspects of life that cannot adequately be conveyed by words. In particular architecture can identify the various stratifications within society, from church and government, the expression of the role of the arts, sport or technology, to the position of the individual in society.

PROGRAMME AND SITE

Architecture responds to three sets of forces: those of the site, the programme and the prevailing culture. The technology used will be that available within the culture.

[1] C. Norberg-Schulz 'Meaning in Architecture' Meaning in Architecture (edited by Jencks and Baird) London 1969 p. 220.

SUMMARY

ORIENTATION AND IDENTITY

In order to comprehend his environment man needs a clear image of his surroundings. These can be understood by man relating himself to nodes, paths and districts.[1] Kevin Lynch lists the three components of an environmental image as being 'identity, spatial context and meaning.'

MOVEMENT

As a component of architecture movement may be thought of as a force having different kinds of intensity. A sports stadium or auditorium is concerned on the one hand with providing the best possible view for spectators and on the other with ensuring their swift and convenient access and egress. An arterial road is a major force in the landscape or city, a force comparable with that of a swift flowing river. The route towards, into and around a building is frequently a starting point for a design.

VIEWS

Similarly views constitute an important force to the architect, who may exploit their presence in his organization of either buildings or cities.

STRUCTURE AND GEOMETRY

Structure may be understood either in terms of the cultural meanings it expresses (as with different interpretations of the column historically) or as a means of creating a sense of the static or dynamic in a building. As an expression of dynamism structure may suggest tautness or elasticity and will often have a rhythmic component as part of its geometry. Geometry is inevitable in architectural organization as the means of ordering a design and relating the parts to one another.

[1] K. Lynch, Op., Cit., p. 7.

2

ASPECTS OF FORM

ARCHITECTURE AND CULTURE

Susanne K. Langer explains how the architect presents an image of a culture:

A culture is made up, factually, of the activities of human being; it is a system of interlocking and intersecting actions, a continuous functional pattern. As such it is, of course, intangible and invisible. It has physical ingredients — artefacts; also physical symptoms — the ethnic effects that are stamped on the human face, known as its 'expression,' and the influence of social conditions on the development, posture and movement of the human body. But all such items are fragments that 'mean' the total pattern of life only to those who are acquainted with it and may be reminded of it. They are ingredients in a culture, not its image.

The architect creates its image: a physically present human environment that expresses the characteristic rhythmic functional patterns which constitute a culture. Such patterns are the alternation of sleep and waking, venture and safety, emotion and calm, austerity and abandon; the tempo, and the smoothness or abruptness of life; the simple forms of childhood and the complexities of full moral stature, the sacramental and the capricious moods that mark a social order, and that are repeated, though with characteristic selection, by every personal life springing from that order.

Susanne K. Langer, Feeling and Form = A Theory of Art, London, 1953. p. 96

Langer continues this argument by asserting that an environment, 'the created space of architecture, is a symbol of functional existence.'[1] She explains that this has nothing to do with convenient arrangement or provident planning. To Langer, the work of architecture.

> does not suggest things to do but embodies the feeling, the rhythm. the passion or sobriety, frivolity or fear with which things at all are done. That is the image of life which is created in buildings; it is the visible semblance of an 'ethnic domain,' the symbol of humanity to be found in the strength and interplay of forms.[2]

Langer goes on to explain how, because we are organisms, our actions and feelings are organic. Our lives have a metabolic pattern consisting of 'Systole, diastole; making, unmaking; crescendo, diminuendo.'[3] There is, as Langer points out, a close parallel between the organic pattern of our lives and the nature of art. 'It is perception moulded by imagination that gives us the outward world we know.'[4] This is how we react to the world and in consequence 'by virtue of our thought and imagination we have not only feelings, but a life of feeling.'[5]

Langer explains how our life of feeling is a 'stream of tensions and resolutions'.[6] In fact, our lives are an interplay of tensions —'actual nervous and muscular tensions taking place in the human organism.'[7] It is because 'art is a symbolic presentation and not a copy of feeling that there can be as much knowledge of feeling projected into the timeless articulated form of a painting, or a stained glass window, or a subtly proportioned Greek temple, as into the flowing forms of music, dance or recitation.'[8]

[1] Ibid., p. 98. [2] Ibid, p. 99. [3] Ibid, p. 99. [4] Ibid, p.372. [5] Ibid, p. 372. [6] Ibid, p. 372. [7] Ibid, p. 372. [8] Ibid, p. 373.

TENSION AND HARMONY

The emotions we experience throughout our 'life of feeling' are translated by the artist to harness the energy of the life situation. As such, the dynamic aspects of life, its drama and excitement combine with those other experiences of peace, sadness, suffering or exhilaration to become part of the artist's expressive palette.

The fact that life does indeed consist largely of Langer's 'tensions and resolutions' means that this is central to existence. The pattern of life has much to do with striving to attain goals or accomplish tasks resulting in a feeling of satisfaction and fulfilment. The desire and conditions which are created in order to reach such goals produce a certain tension. Once achieved there is a feeling of contentment.

These energies receive artistic expression in the major themes of tension and harmony. If tension and harmony are major forces in life and art they are supported by secondary forces also everpresent in each, the rhythms of night and day, the rhythmic flow of blood as it is pumped around the body, the rhythm of the seasons. Such rhythms are also interpreted by the artist or composer in ways appropriate to whatever medium is employed.

VIEW FROM THE SOUTH WEST

pediment
entablature

column

EAST ELEVATION

PLAN

The Thesion Athens 449-444 B.C.

If the overall statement of the Greek temple is one of harmony and unity, this is achieved primarily in the balance inherent in the bi-laterally symmetrical plan.

This unity has within it the opposing tension between the vertical column and horizontal entablature. The composition relies on a powerful rhythmic component with the major columnar rhythm supported by the secondary rhythms of triglyphs and metopes.

The inclined planes of the roof conclude at each end with the pediments, whose oblique planes and triangular formation suggest another kind of energy. As Maurice de Sausmarez has explained, 'diagonals introduce powerful directional impulses, a dynamism which is the outcome of unresolved tendencies towards vertical and horizontal which are held in balanced suspension.'[1] Although somewhat muted in the shallow angle of the temple pediment, this form is as necessary to terminate the composition at its upper extremity as is the stepped base at ground level.

[1] Maurice de Sausmarez, Basic Design: The Dynamics of Visual Form, London, 1964, p.p. 20-22.

PERMANENCE AND HARMONY

Tempietto at S. Pietro in Montorio, Rome. 1502-10.
architect Bramante.

With its circular plan the Tempietto is a centroidal configuration, maintaining a balance of forces. Centroidal bodies suggest repose and stability whereas linear forms imply activity.

The permanence of architecture gives it a special role as the embodiment of 'the rhythmic functional patterns which constitute a culture.' This permanence makes a special demand on the architect to ensure that the work symbolizes the essence of its particular role in such a way that this can be sustained over a period of time.

The theme of harmony, with its implications of order and unity, is of particular importance to architecture, partly because these issues are preferred symbols culturally but also because the permanence of architecture denies a discordant statement. In this, architecture in general separates itself from the other arts, in which a greater degree of imaginative freedom is possible and in which the strident and discordant note may be acceptable.

The harmonic theme has been expressed in different ways during the various periods in different parts of the world. The Italian Renaissance displays a concern for harmony in a broad philosophical sense, and the compositions of Bramante and Raphael gave symbolic expression to belief in a harmonious universe. The centralized plan, used by Leonardo and Michelangelo, gave architectural conviction to this idea, whilst the gentle rhythm of the arcade became another manifestation of the serene tranquillity of the period.

Although the circular plan is the most obvious architectural device to depict harmony, other centroidal configurations such as the square or polygon may also convey this theme.

One of the most complete statements of serenity based on a harmonious geometric arrangement is that of the garden courts and mausoleum of the Taj Mahal at Agra. Four large square courts subdivided into smaller squares front the mausoleum which is positioned centrally on a platform at one end of the main axis of the ensemble.

At the other end of this axis is the great gateway with its own entrance court flanked by two more courts. The secondary axes are terminated by appropriate incidents in an almost totally consistent application of bi-lateral symmetry.

Within the overall symmetry there are subtle contrasts of surface treatment. The hard white marble and rich decoration of the main platform and mausoleum contrasts with the softness of the garden courts, themselves defined axially by the water of the canals. Minarets give vertical punctuation and establish the main space zones.

RIVER JUMNA
main axis

secondary axis

MAIN PLATFORM

MAUSOLEUM

GARDEN COURTS

CANAL

secondary axis

CANAL

GARDEN COURTS

GREAT GATEWAY

LAYOUT PLAN
Taj Mahal, Agra 1632-53

HARMONY BY GEOMETRY

The design principles used in the design of the Taj Mahal are concerned with mass, surface, geometry and the fact that the plan determines the entire arrangement.

We can relate the design of the mausoleum to a series of design maxims set out by Le Corbusier in his theoretical survey Vers une Architecture.

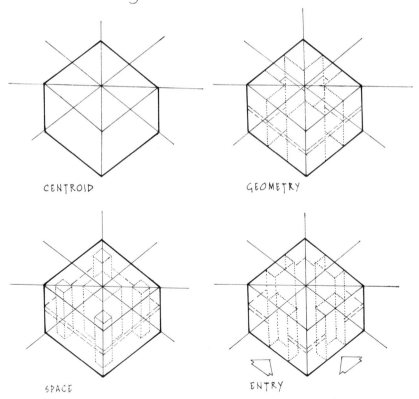

CENTROID

GEOMETRY

SPACE

ENTRY

MASS
'Architecture is the masterly' (stress on the importance of technique) 'correct' (appropriateness of means, method and solution) 'and magnificent play of masses brought together in light.' Forms seen in light because 'Our eyes are made to see forms in light, light and shade reveal these forms; cubes, cones, spheres, cylinders or pyramids are the great primary forms which light reveals to advantage.' [1]

THE PLAN
'The whole structure rises from its base and is developed in accordance with a rule which is written on the ground in the plan...
The plan is at its basis. Without the plan there can be neither grandeur of aim and expression, nor rhythm, nor mass nor coherence. Without plan we have the sensation, so insupportable to man, of shapelessness, of poverty, of disorder, of wilfulness' [2]

GEOMETRY
'But in deciding the form of the enclosure... he has had by instinct recourse to right angles—axes, the square, the circle... For all these things—axes, circles, right angles—are geometrical truths... Geometry is the language of man.' [3]

[1] Le Corbusier Vers une Architecture (translated into English as Towards a new Architecture by Frederick Etchells, London, 1946. p. 31
[2] Ibid., p. 46.   [3] Ibid., p. 68

In his discussion of form, Le Corbusier is at pains to point out that the geometric laws of any particular form should be the basis for subsequent action. Once these geometric laws are understood the various axes can be traced, the properties of forms depending on whether they are linear or centroidal, static or dynamic can be charted. Le Corbusier calls these the 'generating lines' of the form.

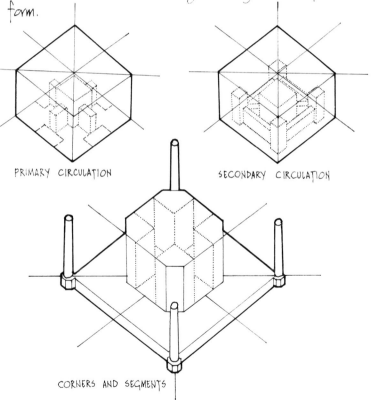

PRIMARY CIRCULATION

SECONDARY CIRCULATION

CORNERS AND SEGMENTS

GENERATING LINES

'If the essentials of architecture lie in spheres, cones and cylinders, the generating and accusing lines of these forms are on a 'basis of pure geometry'.[1]

SURFACE

'To leave a mass intact in the splendour of its form in light, but, on the other hand, to appropriate its surface for needs which are often utilitarian, is to force oneself to discover in this unavoidable dividing up of the surface the <u>accusing</u> and <u>generating</u> lines of the 'form'.[2]

RHYTHM

'Arrangement is an appreciable rhythm which reacts on every human being in the same way.
The plan bears within itself a primary and pre-determined rhythm : . .
Rhythm is a state of equilibrium which proceeds either from symmetries, simple or complex, or from delicate balancings.'[3]

HARMONY

'A profound projection of harmony: this is architecture.'[4]

[1] Ibid., pp. 39, 40.   [2] Ibid., p.p. 37, 39.   [3] Ibid., pp 47, 48.
[4] Ibid., p. 46.

GEOMETRICAL DESIGN

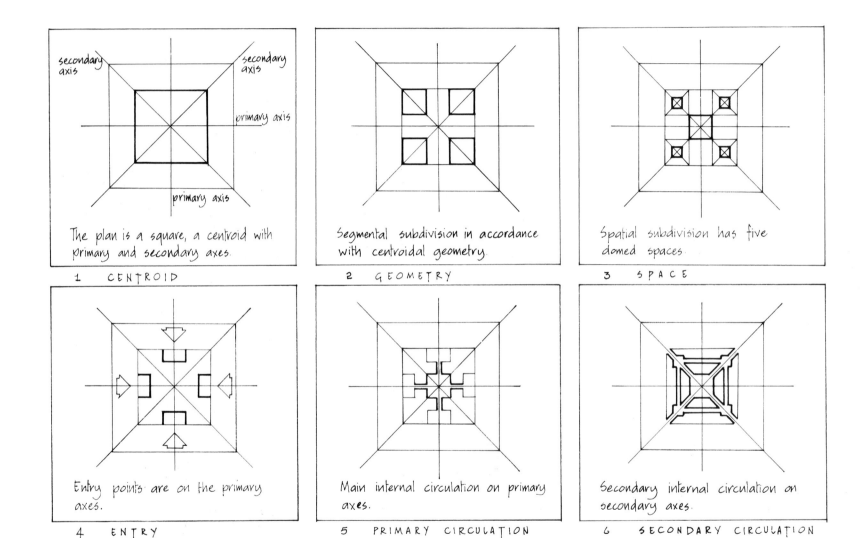

The plan is a square, a centroid with primary and secondary axes.

1   CENTROID

Segmental subdivision in accordance with centroidal geometry.

2   GEOMETRY

Spatial subdivision has five domed spaces.

3   SPACE

Entry points are on the primary axes.

4   ENTRY

Main internal circulation on primary axes.

5   PRIMARY CIRCULATION

Secondary internal circulation on secondary axes.

6   SECONDARY CIRCULATION

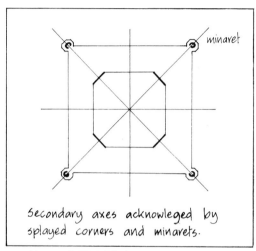

Secondary axes acknowleged by splayed corners and minarets.

7   CORNERS

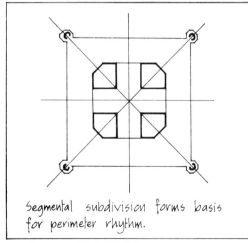

Segmental subdivision forms basis for perimeter rhythm.

8   SEGMENTS

Taj Mahal, Agra   1632-53

Primary and secondary perimeter rhythms.

9   RHYTHMS

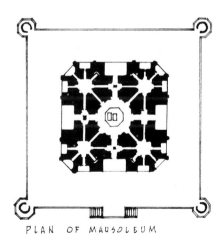

PLAN OF MAUSOLEUM

47

CENTROIDAL STATIC

The Selimiye Mosque Edirne 1568-74 architect Sinan.

CENTROIDAL STATIC

The Taj Mahal, built in the Moghul dynasty, uses the traditional motifs and elements of Islamic architecture. Expressed particularly in the mosques, the architectural language of Islam gives physical expression to the Muslim faith by creating a mood of dignity contemplation and tranquility.

The centralized plan becomes a favourite device, along with the courtyard, domes, arcades and elaborately decorated gateways. It is an architecture of form, space, light and surface decoration which relies on a well established code of authoritative symbols in order to ensure that the buildings are culturally meaningful.

In terms of technique this is an architecture of symmetry controlled by axes. Although the emphasis is on serenity and equilibrium the contrast between the 'soft' domes and rocket-like minarets becomes a powerful device. The silhouette assumes great importance as does rhythmic repetition, whether this be arches in an arcade, a rhythm of windows or of abstract decoration.

LINEAR DYNAMIC

The western equivalent of this serene architecture of the east is that of the Gothic period as demonstrated in the great medieval cathedrals. In some respects the religious requirements are similar in demanding a contemplative and reverential mood, but the western tradition is infused with dynamism; processional needs change the centroidal into a linear response and soaring verticality charges the interior with a majestic and awe-inspiring statement of the power and glory of God.

The structural audacity of the high nave vaults with 'curtain' walls of stained glass supported by flying buttresses creates a feeling of tension and energy, sustained by the vigorous repetition of elements both within and without.

Again axes control the design; again the overall composition resolves its tensions in a state of equilibrium. No less rich or mysterious than their eastern counterpart the cathedrals also rely on a well established architectural language in which form, space, light and decoration convey a range of symbolic intentions.

Chartres Cathedral (rebuilt 1194-1260)

LINEAR DYNAMIC

CHARTRES

vertical force of nave

AISLE
NAVE
AISLE

vertical thrust of towers

clear definition of entry
deep penetration of wall

The plan is linear and directional organised about the main longitudinal axis. The nave is clearly defined, a vertical space with the ridge of the roof confirming the main axis.

The position of entry and rose window reinforce the main axis. Twin towers proclaim the cathedral. The wall between the towers has considerable thickness. As a barrier it has to be penetrated, so entry into the cathedral becomes a significant event marked by three large doorways.

'anchorage' role of towers

vigorous vertical rhythm of flying buttresses oblique angle increases dynamism.

porches amplify entry

steps give added importance to entry

interior vaulting defined by porches

radial system of chevet chapels

The directional thrust of the main longitudinal axis is tempered by a transverse axis. The centre point of the cathedral is established where the axes cross. This has a stabilizing effect, allowing entry through screen walls which confirm the dominant linear theme.

The processional double ambulatory and seven radial chapels provide an appropriate climax to the directional momentum. Surrounding the altar and choir the ambulatory concludes the rich and rhythmic vaulting sequence of the nave, echoed externally by the flying buttresses with their taut outward thrust.

FORCES

THREE POWERFUL DIRECTIONAL THRUSTS
LONGITUDINAL, LATERAL, VERTICAL.

RADIAL RHYTHM OF CHEVET CHAPELS

TOWERS HOLD ENTRY

SIDE PLANES HOLD TRANSVERSE AXIS

CRUDE MASS WITHOUT BUTTRESSES

The Gothic cathedral [1] takes the essential structural forces of wall vault and buttress and by a process of elimination reduces these to maximum visible effectiveness and drama. This is achieved by an accentuation of each potential force opportunity whether these concern the horizontal, vertical or oblique. The resultant total recognition of forces assumes equilibrium within a harmonic plan configuration compacted to maximize the dynamic tension.

OBLIQUE THRUST

VERTICAL RHYTHM OF BUTTRESSES
CURVES AND OBLIQUES
RICH COMPLEXITY OF STRUCTURE
SPACE AROUND FORM MODULATED BY BUTTRESSES
CLOSE COMPACTION INCREASES DYNAMIC TENSION

ORGANIZATION

Erwin Panofski[1] has described how the High Gothic style of the great French cathedrals runs parallel to the development of 'High' Scholasticism, and how these two important events in Western culture emanated during the twelfth century from an area less than a hundred miles around Paris.[2]

Panofski explains how scholars in the twelfth and thirteenth centuries sought to establish the unity of truth.[3] Elucidation or clarification was the controlling principle and for the first time Scholasticism established a logical sequence of division and subdivision in writing so that the reader is led 'step by step from one proposition to the other and is always kept informed of the process.' As Panofski points out, this does not mean that Scholastics were more orderly in their thinking than their predecessors but that they 'felt compelled to make the orderliness and logic of their thought palpably explicit.'[4]

ZONAL ORGANIZATION OF THE GOTHIC CATHEDRAL

This process of clarification and articulation of thought expressed through the written word can also be observed during this period in the organization of pictorial space and in musical notation. It was, however, architecture, with its hierarchy of functional needs, which provided the best opportunity for clear articulation. The Gothic cathedral had an unambiguous zonal distribution of space, with the nave taking precedence over the transepts and aisles, and the choir and chevet chapels acting as the climax to the nave. Processional requirements ensured that axes controlled the arrangement, and structural needs ensured clarity in the rhythmic repetition of vaults and buttresses.

[1] Erwin Panofski, Gothic architecture and scholasticism. New York, 1957.
[2] Ibid., pp. 4,5.   [3] Ibid., p. 28.   [4] Ibid., p. 34.

53

COMPLEXITY AND CONTRADICTION

The explicit clarity of the Gothic style may be compared to that of the Modern Movement in architecture, although the modernists, by substituting abstraction for applied decoration, produced far simpler shapes. This approach emerged from a desire to eliminate 'unnecessary' ornament and to rationalize and 'purify' architecture in terms of new technology and the twentieth century zeitgeist.

Typical of this approach is the work of Le Corbusier, whose output during the twenties proved so influential in propagating the modernist credo. Although Le Corbusier relied heavily on an extensive knowledge of the architecture of the past, he became convinced (partly through this knowledge) that to communicate effectively on an emotional level it was necessary to use primary forms.

However, Le Corbusier's influential book Towards a New Architecture (1923) was followed four decades later by an alternative point of view put by Robert Venturi, who argued against the puritanically moral language of orthodox Modern architecture in postulating an argument for Complexity and Contradiction in Architecture (the title of his seminal study). In an attack on the limited reductionist position adopted by many modernists Venturi explains that he likes 'elements which are hybrid rather than "pure," compromising rather than "clean," distorted rather than "straightforward," ambiguous rather than "articulated," perverse as well as impersonal, boring as well as "interesting," conventional rather than "designed," accommodating rather than excluding, redundant rather than simple, vestigial as well as innovating, inconsistent and equivocal rather than direct and clear. I am for messy vitality over obvious unity. I include the non sequitur and proclaim the duality.'[1]

[1] R. Venturi, Complexity and Contradiction in Architecture, New York, 1966, p. 16.

Villa Savoye Poissy 1929-31
architect Le Corbusier

Porta Pia Rome 1561-64
architect Michelangelo

This tirade, directed at the all too evident sterility of modern architecture, is supported by an extensive discussion in which Venturi draws perceptively on examples from all periods, explaining that both Le Corbusier and Alvar Aalto explored complexity and contradiction in their work.

But it is the architecture of the Baroque and Rococo styles which provide Venturi with some of his best evidence. He contrasts the Modern Movement tendency to prefer consistency between internal arrangement and external expression with the difference between inside and out in certain styles of the past. He explains that such contradictions between inside and out result in a tension between inner and outer form: 'Designing from the outside in, as well as the inside out, creates necessary tensions, which help make architecture. Since the inside is different from the outside, the wall — the point of change — becomes an architectural event. Architecture occurs at the meeting of interior and exterior forces of use and space. These interior and environmental forces are both general and particular, generic and circumstantial. Architecture as the wall between the inside and the outside becomes the spatial resolution of this drama.'[1]

Venturi demonstrates this maxim convincingly in his entrance treatment of the Extension to the National Gallery in London. (see pages 290 and 291).

[1] Ibid. p. 86.

Church of the Concezione at Montecalvario 1718-24
architect Domenico Antonio Vaccaro

THE DYNAMIC ENERGY OF FORM

The vigorous handling of form evident in the Baroque and Rococo styles demonstrates the kind of energy that can be generated in works of architecture. Michelangelo's Porta Pia is but one example from his output to display the dynamism evident in his buildings. The expression of muscularity and power is closely related to these tendencies in his sculpture and painting.

This energy is not however confined to earlier periods and twentieth century architecture has often displayed a dynamic treatment of form, as for example in the work of the Futurists, Constructivists and Expressionists. It is nevertheless the work of certain important architects which most clearly illustrates the tendency, including Luigi Morretti, Hans Scharoun, Alvar Aalto and Le Corbusier. Each distributes this energy in different ways and Aalto frequently uses variations on radial themes as a means by which to induce dynamism.

In Aalto's work the energy is carefully controlled, with forms modulated so as to distribute the energy and at the same time contain it. In the Rovaniemi Library, a typical Aalto format, the linear elements act as a holding baseline, pulling the form out sideways to house administrative accommodation and the lecture hall and ancillary facilities. In contrast, the reading room fans out beyond this, breaking free of the holding boundaries of the form. Functionally this distinction

acknowledges the importance of the reading room as the heart of the library and creates a tension between the prosaic linear form and its radial offshoot.

The points where radial and linear conjoin are treated differently at each end, with an echelon at one side and an abrupt stop at the other. This gives the form directionality so that it can be read as pointing like a pistol.

Within the main shapes Aalto creates supporting shapes so that banks of offices become rhythmic sequences and circulation in the long section reinforces the linearity of the plan, modulating differences between the parts as it meanders alongside them.

The reception desk to the reading room establishes the difference between the two zones by responding to both in its angled shape on plan. This fluency in planning is taken through into the third dimension as the section provides sunken levels, giving greater intimacy in the reading room whilst helping to articulate the radial segments.

Further definition is given by angled light sources which modify the spatial, functional and symbolic role of the reading room.

56

ALVAR AALTO

pistol image

rhythmic offices form holding baseline

directional thrust | linear axis

circulation meander

echelon link

radial reading room

Neue Vahr High Rise Apartments Bremen 1958-62

FIRST FLOOR PLAN

Rovaniemi Library

outer echelon

radial segments

holding zone

Museum of Modern Arts Shiraz Iran 1970 -

CROSS SECTIONS THROUGH READING ROOM (ABOVE)
AND THROUGH GALLERY (BELOW)

THE CLASSIC WORK

If we attempt to identify those characteristics that define the classic work, that take it beyond the ordinary, we may outline the following as being present in the major work; 1) a mastery of technique; 2) exceptional composition; 3) an enduring quality; 4) authority; 5) either abstractly or directly, some reference to our experience of life.

Each of the arts deals with these criteria in ways that are appropriate to our sensory apparatus. Music and literature, for example, may nurture our imagination so that we respond to sounds and words by picturing something in the mind's eye. Music, in particular, can directly affect our emotions and its rhythms may be associated with the rhythmic coursing of the blood or the rhythm of the days and seasons. Painting explores the way we enjoy colour, shape and arrangement, whilst the poet might engage subtle areas of meaning that are most readily conveyed by words. Architecture involves all our senses, as for example when we walk through a courtyard with a fountain and trees. We are aware of sounds, shapes, proportions, scale, texture and pattern. We may also be subjected to a series of impressions, concerned with intimacy, privacy, power, wealth or poverty. A courtyard may have historic associations; it may suggest academia, the church or government.

If we take the above criteria in turn, they have specific implications for each of the arts:

MASTERY OF TECHNIQUE

Although technique may be taken for granted in the arts, an enhanced level of quality may be given to major works by absolute mastery of technique. This implies mastery of the means by which intentions may be accomplished. The composer of a musical score must be familiar with the various instruments to have the necessary control of expression. In architecture such control is associated with knowledge of materials and constructional technology. The work of a master such as Alvar Aalto is exemplary in the way every detail, from window mullion to door handle, informs the final building.

EXCEPTIONAL COMPOSITION

The major work will be understood as such in part by its arrangement — in music of sounds, in poetry of words, in architecture by the articulation of the various elements. Such compositions may be rich and elaborate as in opera, or quite simple as in some poems and works of art. Because of its nature and life-expectancy, architectural arrangements may tend towards order and symmetry, or alternatively towards a dynamic balance of contrasting elements.

Robert Venturi has shown [1] that architecture can be complex, ambiguous and contradictory. He quotes examples from Mannerist and Baroque architecture in which the level of elaboration sets out to confound the usual expectations. Within necessary limits of comfort, structure and weather-proofing, such strategies impart that vitality which emerges in certain periods as a reaction against what has gone before. This oscillation, from the staid to the lively, from serenity to vigorous dramatisation and even confusion, exemplifies the way in which the arts renew themselves in response to changing cultural circumstances.

AN ENDURING QUALITY

This is found in major works in the way that we can return to them again and again, to discover something fresh or to be reacquainted with familiar qualities. In fulfilling

[1] Robert Venturi, Complexity and Contradiction in Architecture, New York, 1966.

THE CLASSIC WORK

this requirement the major work may be complex or simple. Different kinds of complexity and simplicity create this enduring quality in each of the arts. The orchestral symphony consists of several contrasting but related movements; the novel consists of a series of related chapters. In each case a theme or story unfolds in a continuous linear fashion. In contrast architecture is usually perceived as a whole, albeit consisting of a series of related parts. These may also be experienced sequentially by movement through a building.

Architecture may be complex, as for example in Richard Meier's Atheneum,[1] or relatively simple as in Bramante's Tempietto.[2] But architecture's practical and symbolic role seldom allows the kind of freedom enjoyed by the painter or musician. It is difficult to imagine an architectural equivalent to the random complexity of a Jackson Pollock painting, although Watts Towers in Los Angeles come fairly close.

Order and clarity are almost always important considerations in architecture. The need to communicate meaning usually demands a consensus architecture in which the familiarity of the language ensures shared comprehension. By this means certain styles persist, whether in civic or domestic buildings. In the sixteenth century, Andrea Palladio evolved an architectural style which has persisted to the present day. The reason for this enduring quality (as found in his Villa Capra)[3] lies in a blend of simplicity and complexity, together with the architect's careful manipulation of the communicative aspect. Palladio creates forms that are simple enough to cause no perceptual difficulties — his forms can readily be understood as wholes — they observe time-honoured architectural canons of order and symmetry, yet are embellished with meaningful decoration in the form of classical motifs. Palladio fully understood the nature of architecture, an understanding which drew extensively on Greek and Roman precedent.

[1] see pages 187-231
[2] see page 42
[3] see page 14

AUTHORITY

To have authority, the work must inspire a confidence based on the author's command of his medium. Again this will have a different inference for each of the arts. Our confidence in Shakespeare stems from the conviction apparent in his portrayals and characterizations. Consummate technique and impeccable composition contribute, but his authority is due to a universal recognition of his mastery of every aspect of his art.

This is also the case with architecture. Authority resides in total conviction. This is particularly evident in certain periods in which every aspect of the architectural phenomenon is resolved. Kings' College Chapel, Cambridge is such an example. A complete work, which integrates structure, form, proportions, decorative treatment and lighting in a way that expresses spirituality and which is perfectly at one with it's setting. Such are the demands on architecture and architects that this fusion is difficult to attain and is apparent in the great periods which represent a summation of man's progress. When this occurs architecture adds authority to the purpose it serves.

On another level, vernacular architecture, or the architecture of popular taste, will have its own authority when it embraces all man's needs, practical and symbolic. In popular, universal stereotypes of domestic habitation, found in all parts of the world, authority resides in the complete rapport between programme, climate and culture. In such stereotypes, structure, materials, craftsmanship, economic forces and symbolism are all combined in a manner that emerges through the roots of the culture. This recognizes the importance of tradition, the common perceptions of status and conformity and the need to convey meanings shared by all. As with a Rembrandt portrait or a Beethoven symphony, there is a concern for universal truths which transcend fashion, superficiality or contrivance. The fact that architecture is all-embracing and deals with so many aspects of existence means that it is extremely difficult for an individual architect to produce work of real authority.

THE CLASSIC WORK

REFERENCE TO THE EXPERIENCE OF LIFE

This discussion has already indicated the extent to which the major work will illuminate our perception of life. The artist, author, composer or architect will draw out and reconstitute significant aspects of experience. The way this is done will depend on the capacity of the medium, which will also determine the subject matter. Degas' portrayals of dancers heighten our perception of dance, they convey the beauty of the female form and how this may be enhanced by costume, lighting and choreography.

As the framework for existence, architecture participates directly in life, and as an art form it is assessed as to the extent to which it enhances and enriches life. The close connection with practical and symbolic issues separates architecture from the other arts which may seek to inform or entertain. Architecture has a particularly responsible role, allowing less licence or self-indulgence than the other arts. It is most successful when it absorbs the life forces so that they are correctly assimilated. A staircase or stair handrail must be correctly shaped to permit easy and comfortable movement. In this sense architecture is anthropomorphic – this is its connection with life. Similarly in providing shelter, comfort and order architecture directly addresses the concerns of life. Its authority and conviction depend on this ability to satisfy practical and emotional needs.

This may be manifest in subtle ways. Barry and Pugin's Palace of Westminster contains two strands of the British Parliament, the Houses of Lords and Commons. This division, separating the aristocracy from the commoner, reflects a British societal tradition. As an expression of this, the Gothic style refers to the historic continuity which the building represents. In straddling the arts and sciences, aesthetics and practicality; in dealing with symbolism and a communicative consensus, representing cultural continuity and the present, architecture expresses aspects of life directly. Like major works in the other arts, the major work of architecture will reveal a comprehensive understanding of all those life forces which must be absorbed and encapsulated in built form.

3

THE ANALYSIS OF ARCHITECTURE

ANALYSIS

This analytical methodology seeks to discover those primary organizational factors which operate in a building or project, and in so doing to reveal the preoccupations of the designer. This is done by a process of dissection which charts the existence of such factors as volumetric disposition (including the kind of geometrical system used), the circulation pattern (in many cases directly linked to the volumetric disposition) the location of key axes, both within the building and in the immediate proximity, and (where relevant) the structural system. The relevance to the general organization of the materials used, environmental considerations (sun control, prevention of heat loss or excessive gain) and the arrangement of services may also be taken into account.

These factors are analyzed with reference to the purpose which the building is intended to serve, and to the kind of symbolic imagery which the building seeks to express. The analysis also takes account, again where appropriate, of cultural, technological and economic factors.[1]

An important feature of this analytical methodology is the way a building is considered in relation to its site. Site forces[2] such as the presence of a river or other topographical factors, are charted and the building's axes are related to other axes in the vicinity.

[1] It has to be stressed that analysis is a selective, subjective exercise. In this study emphasis is given to the analysis of architectural form, and only issues central to this intention are considered. Essentially any analytical investigation will focus on those issues considered specifically relevant to the subject matter. It follows from this that no two analyses will necessarily be alike, in treatment or in the emphasis given to each area under discussion.

[2] The term forces is used to indicate a weighting, a degree of intensity or energy emanating from the source. This will exert an influence on its surroundings, depending on its strength, usage, power of massing or means of making its presence felt in a situation.

The analysis relates the site forces (which include orientation, views and access), to those organizational forces identified within the building. The analysis seeks to discover how the building is conceived in relation to its site.[1] To be of most value in terms of the concerns of this study, the analysis will usually examine a major work, the task being, as far as possible, to reveal those intuitive processes which have guided the designer.

As in literary or musical analysis, major themes are sought within the work and then examined to see whether or not they are carried through consistently.[2]

[1] See G.H. Baker 'Chichester College Revisited' R.I.B.A. Journal, November 1980, pp 45-47. Also videos 'Chichester Theological College' produced by Media Services, Brighton Polytechnic. and 'The Atheneum, an analysis of form' produced and directed by Gordon Brooks, University of Arkansas, 1988. (Distributed by the University of California at Los Angeles).

[2] See Geoffrey Baker, Le Corbusier: An analysis of form. (Third Edition, 1996) E. and F.N. Spon, London.

DIAGRAMMATIC THOUGHT

Diagrams are the essential tool of both analyst and designer. Their use encourages thought patterns capable of considerable dexterity. This dexterity, the ability to grasp the essence of a concept, and through this understanding to fully develop an idea, is central to the act of design.

DIAGRAMS:

ARE SELECTIVE

ARE ABOUT CLARITY AND COMMUNICATION

REVEAL THE ESSENCE

ARE OFTEN SIMPLE

SEPARATE OUT ISSUES SO AS TO COMPREHEND THE COMPLEX

MAKE GEOMETRIC ARTICULATION EXPLICIT

CAN QUANTIFY THE ENERGY IN BOTH SITE AND CONCEPT

ALLOW A DEGREE OF ARTISTIC LICENCE

CAN HAVE A VITALITY OF THEIR OWN

CAN EXPLAIN FORM AND SPACE BETTER THAN WORDS OR PHOTOGRAPHS

RIVER WEAR

TOPOGRAPHY

R O U T E S   **C I R C U L A T I O N   P A T T E R N**

An understanding of city structure can be gained by charting topography
routes and circulation patterns. The city of Durham was built on the high
ground of a peninsula formed by the river Wear. To the north a convergence
of routes established the market place, commanded by the high ground of
the castle mound. The steep banks of the river create a natural defensive
barrier and on the high plateau to the south of the castle the cathedral
dominates the city, its east/west axis running counter to the north/south
axis of the peninsula.

64

SLAB TRANSFORMED

Le Corbusier's Villa Stein-de-Monzie can be diagrammatically explained as a series of transformations of a rectilinear slab.

RECTILINEAR BOX

BASIC GEOMETRY

FORM ERODED AND DISTORTED

EROSION CORRECTED
CASCADING TERRACES

HORIZONTAL AND VERTICAL PLANES

GEOMETRIC CONTROL

Although this analytical study does not set out to show how Le Corbusier evolved his design concept, this kind of dissection highlights issues of concern to him when the villa was designed. In this way analysis can reveal strategies and tactics used by an architect.[1]

DISTORTION ACKNOWLEDGED

EROSION COUNTERED

SYMMETRY

ASYMMETRY

BALANCE

LINKAGES

[1] For a detailed analysis of the villa see Geoffrey H. Baker, Le Corbusier: An analysis of Form. (Third Edition, 1996) E. and F. N. Spon, London.

GENERIC AND SPECIFIC FORM

Architectural form may be thought of as generic, in its original state, and specific, when the form assumes finality having been manipulated and organized to satisfy the functional demands of the programme and the particular confines or opportunities presented by the site.

Peter Eisenman has explained [1] how, when we read a square with one of its corners cut away, this is read in terms of its gestalt, as a square, which becomes the generic antecedent of the form.

Forms can be understood in relation to their generic antecedent, as when the articulation of the Monastery of St. Marie de La Tourette derives from a generic courtyard origin.

Similarly the Villa Capra may be read in terms of its square generic antecedent, reversing the courtyard of La Tourette with a centroidal core. As Eisenman points out, 'form in its generic state will provide the conceptual reference for all physical manifestations of specific form as well as give the basis for the specific ordering of this form. Form thought of in its conceptual state must acknowledge the requirements of the generic conditions.' [2]

[1] P. Eisenman, The Formal Basis of Modern Architecture, Doctoral dissertation, University of Cambridge, 1963, p. 43.
[2] Ibid., p. 42.

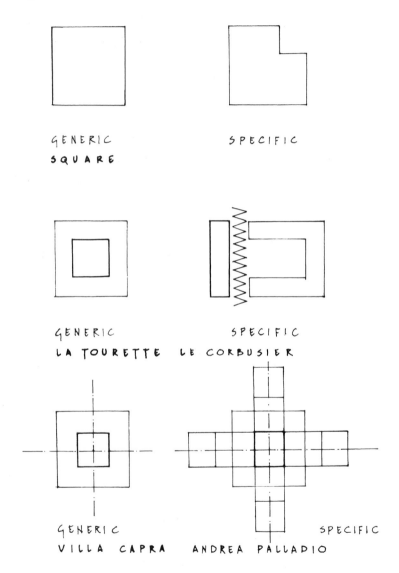

GENERIC
SQUARE

SPECIFIC

GENERIC
LA TOURETTE

SPECIFIC
LE CORBUSIER

GENERIC
VILLA CAPRA

SPECIFIC
ANDREA PALLADIO

The Monastery of La Tourette derives its conceptual origin from the square courtyard plan of the Cistercian monastic complex.[1] This generic form is changed by the interrelation between site forces and programmatic requirements.

From the generic square courtyard, site characteristics induce a linear condition. The program identifies a specific role for the church which is separated from the rest of the configuration. For functional and symbolic reasons the monks cells are arranged in a pinwheel formation and a linear route gives access from the monastic accommodation to the church.

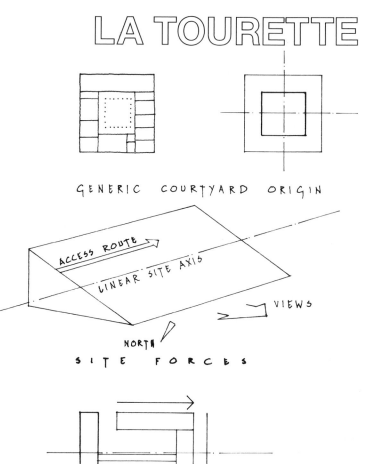

GENERIC COURTYARD ORIGIN

SITE FORCES

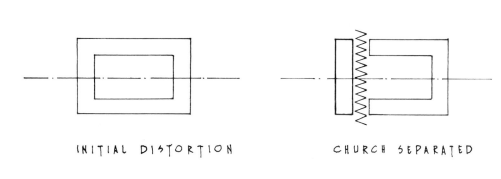

INITIAL DISTORTION

CHURCH SEPARATED

CELLS PINWHEEL AND LINEAR ROUTE

[1] Father Coutourier, acting as client for the monastery, sent Le Corbusier a sketch of the plan of a traditional Cistercian monastery. For an analysis of the design see G.H. Baker, Le Corbusier: An analysis of form (Third Edition, 1996) E. and F. N. Spon, London.

CARTESIAN GRID AND HORIZONTAL ABSOLUTE

Peter Eisenman refers to the three dimensional cartesian grid as 'the absolute reference for architectural form whether generic or specific.[1]' He explains how this grid of horizontals and verticals refers to the force of gravity and that 'everything is seen with reference to this grid whether man-made or natural.'[2]

In his study of the Greek temple temenos <u>The idea of space in Greek architecture</u>, Dr. Peter Martiensen refers to the horizontal absolute, as exemplified by the Greek temple platform, the flat plane on which the temple stands. The horizontal platform features strongly in the work of Jorn Utzen, particularly in his Sydney Opera House where the shells and structure rise from a horizontal podium.

In Le Corbusier's work, curved walls are frequently tensioned against an orthogonal grid, as in the Chapel at Ronchamp. In the case of both Richard Meier's and Le Corbusier's work, the orthogonal cage serves to discipline the organisation of elements. (see analysis of Meier's Atheneum, pp. 192-231)

CARTESIAN GRID

HORIZONTAL ABSOLUTE

[1] Peter Eisenman, <u>The formal basis of modern architecture</u>, Doctoral dissertation, University of Cambridge, 1963. p. 27
[2] Ibid, p 28

72

Chapel at Ronchamp 1950-55
architect Le Corbusier

Sydney Opera House 1943 architect Jorn Utzon

MASS AND SURFACE

For analytical purposes it is important to distinguish between mass and surface. Mass may be regarded as the solid component of form as exemplified in Palladio's Villa Capra at Vicenza. In contrast, Le Corbusier's studio/apartment for Amadeé Ozenfant in Paris may be seen as a statement of planes.

In general Alvar Aalto states mass in his projects (see analysis of Säynätsalo, pp. 159-185) whereas Mies van de Rohe is concerned with a juxtaposition of planes. The Barcelona Pavilion may be regarded as the antithesis of Palladio's mass statements in masonry, this being a consequence of the availability of steel and large glazed areas, coupled with a changed view of spatial composition due partly to the influence of modern art.

Villa Capra Vicenza 1564 architect Andrea Palladio

Barcelona Pavilion 1929 architect Ludwig Mies van de Rohe

Studio apartment for Ozenfant 1922 architect Le Corbusier

Humana Building Louisville Kentucky 1982
architect Michael Graves

Generic rectilinear slab.

Top added to terminate the slab and also to enrich the skyline.

Roof garden and cantilever trusses assist the vertical termination and give a view towards the river.

Lower section in scale with street.

Symmetrical form requires more axial definition and reference to internal functions.

Vertical elements emphasise axiality and tie top and bottom together.

Major openings identify main spaces within the building.

Final articulation responds to context and internal functions using Graves' base shaft and capital system.

75

CENTROIDAL AND LINEAR FORM

Centroidal configurations such as the sphere and the cube maintain a balance of forces as distinct from linear configurations in which the predominant force has a particular energy and direction.

Centroidal bodies suggest repose and stability whereas linear forms imply activity.

Frank Lloyd Wright's Robie house deploys two linear forms in a potentially shifting relationship.

Andrea Palladio's Villa Capra is an almost symmetrical centroid.

About the dynamics of form Maurice de Sausmarez has written

The simplest unit, a spot, not only indicates location but is felt to have within itself potential energies of expansion and contraction which activate the surrounding area. When two spots occur there is a statement of measurement and implied direction and the 'inner' energies create a specific tension between them which directly affects the intervening space.

A line can be thought of as a chain of spots joined together. It indicates position and direction and has within itself a certain energy, the energy to travel along its length and to be intensified at either end, speed is implied and the space around it is activated. In a limited way it is capable of expressing emotions, e.g. a thick line is associated with boldness, a straight line with strength and stability, a zig-zag with excitement.

Horizontals and verticals operating together introduce the principle of balanced oppositions of tensions. The vertical expresses a force which is of primary significance - gravitational pull, the horizontal again contributes a primary sensation - a supporting flatness; the two together produce a deeply satisfying resolved feeling, perhaps because they symbolise the human experience of absolute balance, of standing erect on level ground.

Diagonals introduce powerful directional impulses, a dynamism which is the outcome of unresolved tendencies towards vertical and horizontal which are held in balanced suspension.

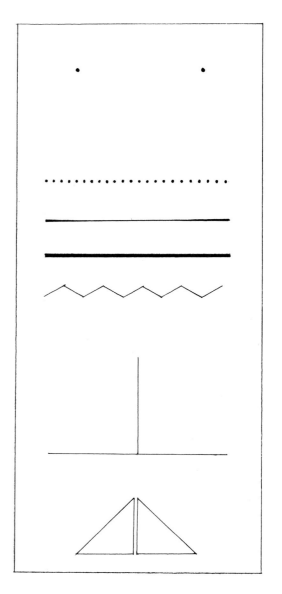

Maurice de Sausmarez, Basic Design: The Dynamics of Visual Form, Studio Vista, London 1964 pp 20-22. by permission of The Herbert Press Ltd.

CORE SYSTEMS

Architectonic arrangements may be described as systems in which the various parts are organised in relation to a thematic idea. The inherent structural nature of architecture implies a geometric organization and the systemic ordering of architectonic form is therefore geometrical.

Centroidal core systems include the spiral - often expressed as a pinwheel - cluster and cruciform systems.

Systems provide a discipline rather than a limit. They allow for growth, they accommodate the scherzo : They can be elaborated to encompass infinite variations and complexities.

Peter Eisenman

core   cluster

pinwheel   cruciform

cruciform system   Ward Willitts house : Frank Lloyd Wright.

pinwheel system   Arthur Heurtley house : Frank Lloyd Wright.

Linear systems afford additive opportunities along axes.
This allows for repetition and the development of rhythms.
Movement becomes an important component of the form.

James Stirling   Residential expansion for St. Andrews University 1964

AXIAL SYSTEMS

Axial ordering has formed the basis of monumental architecture since ancient times. Bi-lateral symmetry with a hierarchical volumetric arrangement was the main organizational system prior to the twentieth century. During the present century axes have also played a key role in the design strategies of many architects.

Temple of Khons Karnak B.C. 1200

Frank Lloyd Wright Darwin D. Martin house 1904

James Stirling's History Faculty Library at Cambridge has a radial plan for the main reading room. This becomes polygonal at the perimeter and entry to the reading room is by an echelon system.

James Stirling Cambridge University History Faculty Building 1964

Aalto's Art Museum at Aalborg has an echeloned entry system within an overall orthogonal grid.

Alvar Aalto Art Museum Aalborg 1969-73

81

INTERLOCKING SYSTEMS

INTERLOCK

GENERIC

SPECIFIC

Unity Church posed a problem for Frank Lloyd Wright in the way to relate the square church to the rectilinear ancillary accommodation. The architect resolves this by locking the two forms together by extending the side walls to the terraces. In his elemental organization Wright observes the geometric properties of the generic forms.

Frank Lloyd Wright   Unity Church   Oak Park   Illinois   1906

FORM DISTORTION

Alvar Aalto's Cultural Centre at Wolfsburg is concerned with a centroidal problem on a linear site. The generic core form is distorted by the site to become rectilinear and in specific terms the form responds radially to the piazza by the arrangement of lecture theatres.

LINEAR SITE

internal site axis

external site axis

GENERIC FORM   DISTORTION

external site axis

SPECIFIC FORM

internal site axis

external site axis

PIAZZA   LECTURE THEATRES

Alvar Aalto Cultural Centre Wolfsburg West Germany 1958-63

PART TWO

ANALYTICAL STUDIES

4
THE VILLAGE AND CITY IN HISTORY

MONASTIC COMPLEX AT ASSISI

At Assisi site forces and programmatic requirements have conspired to create that total architecture so often realized in the Middle Ages. The site comprises a narrow finger of land jutting out from the long hill on which the town of Assisi stands. The monastery has two churches at its core and is linked to the town by two piazze, sculpted into the contours and providing a gap between sacred and secular. This particular problem, in this particular setting, has produced a profound synthesis, in which the monastery, the context, symbolism and cultural values are articulated in an architectural masterpiece.

GENERIC FORM

river

the church

the town

The church to the monastery at Assisi is placed within a linear
site context at the end of the hill on which the town stands
the generic form is linear with a dominant longitudinal axis
A series of routes lead from the monastery to the town and beyond.

The above and following drawings in this sequence are after drawings by Simon Buckley

The generic linear configuration is modulated in accordance with programme and site.
In specific terms two churches are provided, an upper and
a lower, each on different levels.

SPECIFIC FORM

lower church

upper church

Transepts are provided for functional reasons and the plan is organized in accord with symbolic, structural, processional and accommodation requirements.

lower church

In the lower church the main longitudinal axis is tempered by the location of entry to the side, by the axes formed by the transepts and by the provision of extra chapels. The symmetrical gable to the upper church emphasizes its axiality. This entry plane identifies the building within a generally understood code.

95

FORM AS SIGNAL

The campanile acts as a beacon, proclaiming the nature of the activities taking place within the complex.   A porch defines the entry point to the lower church.   The approaches from the town follow the contours at different levels.

FORM AS SYMBOL

The two piazze divide the town from the monastery, a complete symbolic break between secular and holy ground. The piazze enable a full appreciation of the position of the buildings in the landscape, whilst the facade and campanile signify the religious identity of the complex.

WARKWORTH, NORTHUMBERLAND

A universe created by man and for man, 'In the image of nature'... not, indeed by simulating natural objects, but by exemplifying 'the laws of gravity, of statics and dynamics' ... is the spatial semblance of a world, because it is made in actual space, yet is not systematically continuous with the rest of 'nature' in a complete democracy of places. It has its own center and periphery, not dividing one place from all others, but limiting from within whatever there is to be. That is the image of an ethnic domain, the primary illusion in architecture.[1]

[1] Suzanne K. Langer, Feeling and Form, London, 1953, p. 97.

GENIUS LOCI AND SITE FORCES

GENIUS LOCI

Warkworth is situated in Northumberland at the northeastern tip of England. The surrounding countryside is characterized by gently rolling hills and valleys. There is a freshness about this well treed landscape blessed with considerable natural beauty. The area has less rainfall than some parts of England, with a cool climate in which winds from the south west and sometimes from the east blow for much of the year. A lasting impression of the region is of clouds scurrying across a great expanse of sky, green fields, surging rivers and a strong presence of the nearby North Sea with its sandy beaches and dune-edged coastline.

SITE FORCES

The Genius Loci of this particular location is created by specific topographical features. A bend of the river Coquet encloses a piece of land large enough for a settlement. At the narrower neck a mound rises to dominate the terrain with views on all sides. The river is the major force, the mound no less important, with man's intervention in the form of a route leading north towards Scotland and south towards Newcastle-upon-Tyne. A smaller plateau rises alongside the river to the north alongside which a bridge continues the route. Route, mound, river and the 'enclosed' piece of land suggest a 'vocation' for the kind of settlement realized in the form of a medieval village with protective castle.

Drawings in this sequence and up to page 127 are after drawings by Simon Buckley.

VIEWS

VIEWS

TO SCOTLAND

RIVER COQUET

NORTH

TO THE SOUTH AND NEWCASTLE-UPON-TYNE

The bend of the river dominated by a mound.
provides a defensive location.
An artificial ditch separates the mound from adjacent land.
A castle is built on the mound with extensive views on all sides.
The bridge 'gathers' space on each side of the river and is
a major linear manifestation of the route.
The river, the mound with its views, and the route, are the main forces.

CULTURAL FACTORS AND MATERIALS

CULTURAL FACTORS

The favoured defensive location almost certainly means that man would have settled in Warkworth in pre-medieval times. The mound was an ideal location for a 'motte and bailey' castle, this being first mentioned in 1158. At Warkworth the bailey enclosure was placed to the south and a stone keep was built on the motte dominating the higher northern side. At the opposite end a ditch protects the castle against attack from the south. Castles were an integral and necessary part of the feudal system, a system in which the king had control of much of the country, the rest being maintained by barons in return for agreed services to the crown. In 1332 Warkworth was granted to Henry, second Lord Percy of Alnwick, and the Percy's built the present tower house to replace the earlier keep. (1380-90)

A small village formed on either side of the north/south route with feudal strip plots leading down to the river on either side. A church was built on an east-west axis on the small mound to the north with space around it for a graveyard. The main street is too confined for a market place so a small square is formed adjacent on the south side of the church.

MATERIALS

The use of stone, with its implications of strength leading to security, gives a monumental character to both castle and church. Stone is also used for the dwellings in the town, increasing the homogeneity of the whole.

Feudal strip plots form a settlement
on either side of the route.
A church is built on an east/west
axis on the northern mound.
A market place is formed in front
of the church.
The long side of the church blocks
the end of the main street.

CASTLE

MARKET PLACE

CHURCH

STRIP PLOTS

RIVER COQUET

RELEVANT ISSUES

MEANING AND POETRY

Thus church and castle form an axis, marked by their towers. Castle, town and church form a **homogeneous** and self-contained world at a time when this would be the only world its inhabitants would know. The architecture 'concretises' the shared meanings of this society and Heidegger's poetic dimension is realised in the fusion between man's activities and nature, achieved so as to gather the properties of the place.

PROGRAMME, SITE, IDENTITY

Here the program may be said to be the need for **defence**, a place to dwell, and spiritual sustenance. These needs are met by an architectural response to the site and the prevailing culture. Regarding orientation, the environmental image has identity in the form of castle, **village** and church.

MOVEMENT AND GEOMETRY, MONUMENTAL AND VERNACULAR

In the form of the route, movement becomes a prime generator of the complex. Both castle (the keep) and church may be thought of as monumental architecture with a simple vernacular model comprising **the village**. Castle and church have a geometric form as befits both their structural requirements and symbolic role whilst the bridge has a pronounced linearity signalling arrival from the north much as the castle heralds arrival from the south. This clarification of boundaries already formed by the river increases the sense of protection and security so necessary at this near-border location.

RIVER COQUET

sketch from church door.

CAMPO AND CATHEDRAL, SIENA

The beauty of Siena is not merely the result of an unconscious or 'natural' growth; it has been consciously built up by its citizens, as a work of art, with a keen sense of unity but also with that deep respect for the inherited rights of the castes, the professions, and the clans, which is the special mark of the Middle Ages... in France and in Germany the northern Gothic period produced the cathedral as its masterpiece, Italy in the Middle Ages reached the height of communal achievement in the building of the Gothic town. [1]

The evolution of Siena typifies how religious faith, economic forces, city rivalry and a capacity to exploit the Genius Loci conspired to create a series of masterly towns and cities in Italy during the Middle Ages.

Siena, Florence and Pisa each struggled to retain the trade route between France and Rome as it passed through Tuscany. Pisa's importance lay with its harbour, and Florence was favourably located on the river Arno, but with the sea abandoning Pisa, the main rivalry was between Florence and Siena.

Throughout the 12th century the Tuscany trade route had been controlled by Siena, this **being due** in large **measure** to the trading success of the city. The resultant conflict led to war between the rival cities and to victory for the Sienese in 1262 at Montaperto.

[1] Titus Burckhardt, Siena, The City of the Virgin, London, 1960, p. 1

CULTURE AND SITE

In the 12th century the present Campo was an open space facing south, defined by a conjunction of routes and contours. Due to erosion by rain a retaining wall was built to the south, and in 1218 a master plan for the piazza was initiated. In 1288 all the houses around the square were acquired by the City with additional houses purchased in 1293.

A cathedral had been built on a hill to the west of the Campo in 1216. In 1339 it was decided to begin building a new cathedral with an extension of the chancel in the form of a new nave, running north-south. With the intervention of the 'Black Death' and escalating costs this had to be abandoned and the existing building was retained with certain ongoing additions. These included a new Baptistery, built on the lower slope beneath the cathedral choir, and a new facade, modelled on the facade of Orvieto cathedral and completed in 1377.

A new Town Hall was begun in 1297, sited in what was then the market place and which is now the Campo. The Town Hall had to face the cathedral and had to be built at the southern side of the market place. In 1297, following this decision, it was decreed that in order to create a harmonious whole all windows looking on to the Campo should be adorned with small columns. [1]

[1] Ibid., p. 24.

In the medieval city the need for protection was primarily expressed in two ways. Fortified walls provided a defensive ring around the city, and the cathedral acted as the source of contact with God, the ultimate guardian of destiny. At the height of its greatest flowering, during the 12th, 13th and 14th centuries, the inhabitants described Siena as the City of the Virgin, and the Cathedral and Town Hall symbolized the religious and temporal power of the city.

The Cathedral hovers over the city like a huge black and white striped airship, whilst lower down the slopes, nestling into the hillside, the Piazza del Campo with its Town Hall, acts as a stage for public events, its campanile rising bravely into the sky, proclaiming the civic pride of the city.

DUOMO

CAMPO

MARKET PLACE

Topography and routes conjoin to establish a node which, over time, has produced not only a remarkable piazza, but which has also managed to represent symbolically the relationship between church, public life and commerce, by the location of the Cathedral, Campo and market place.

GROSSETO

SAN GIMIGNANO

DUOMO

FLORENCE

CAMPO

ROME

NORTH

MAIN ROUTES WITHIN THE FORTIFIED WALLS OF SIENA.

115

CAMPO

Siena stands on a series of ridges, along
which are the main routes to Florence, San
Gimignano, Grosseto and Rome.

At the heart of the old city is the Piazza
del Campo. From the earliest days this was
a place where travellers would rest on the
way to and from neighbouring cities.

Campo means 'an open field' and is located between
the ridges along which the main routes through
Sienna conjoin. Views from the enclosed Campo
are along the valley whose main axis runs
through the campo.

SAN GIMIGNANO

FLORENCE

GROSSETO

CAMPO

VALLEY

AXIS OF VALLEY

VALLEY

NORTH

ROME

116

The natural enclosure given by the contours is confirmed
by the buildings which enclose the Campo. This crescent
shape sets up an axis which follows the axis of the
valley.

The enclosed space is both inward and outward looking,
with a central focal point and views down the valley.

114

DIAGONAL AXIS

VIEW FROM SOUTH WEST

The need for a link between the Cathedral and the Piazza del Campo is accommodated by the only major break in the buildings surrounding the square. This occurs on the western side, establishing a diagonal axis across the Campo.

VIEW FROM SOUTH EAST

PALAZZO PUBBLICO

The Town Hall, or Palazzo Pubblico closes the southern side of the piazza, being formed of three segments which bend round to echo the shell-like sense of enclosure within the Campo.

view of tower from passage A

egress points to Market Square

passage A

The Torre del Mangia is placed on the eastern side of the Palazzo, forming a visual stop for the oblique axis across the square. Of six secondary points of access to the space, the two open to the sky give views onto the tower whilst three others look towards the central section of the Palazzo Pubblico.

The Torre del Mangia, as the only vertical element in the square, acts as a powerful signal, with its most elaborate treatment reserved for the top, which can be seen for miles. The clock is pulled down to relate to the piazza, of which it forms a part.

The containment on the south side of the piazza retains the focal effect and represents the importance of civic life by the pyramidal build-up and bi-lateral symmetry of the Town Hall.

MARKET

view down valley

To the rear of the Palazzo Pubblico is a loggia which enjoys a view of the valley and which relates directly to the market.

At the focal point within the square is the storm drain on which the various radii of the Campo converge, these reinforcing the fan-like nature of the space and also helping to unify the piazza. Centrally on axis is the Fonte Gaia, the fountain placed low so as not to interfere with the space in the square.

If we think of the Piazza del Campo as an outdoor auditorium, the Palazzo Pubblico seems like a scene building fronted by a stage for public events. The porch at the base of the tower states its position in relation to the square much as the upper part establishes the tower and Palazzo to distant horizons.

The porch also acts as a visual stop at eye level to the oblique axis across the piazza.

The way the floor of the piazza slopes down to the storm drain intensifies the feeling of enclosure on three sides, this being confirmed by the presence of the Town Hall on the other.

Taking a section through the Campo shows that entrances from the north do not reveal the full extent of the space initially, unlike the view from the main entry point.

view into piazza restricted from northern entrances.

storm drain

During the day the shadow of the tower moves around the square like a giant sun dial.

SECTION THROUGH CAMPO

ROUTES

route begins   CAMPO

CATHEDRAL

MARKET PLACE

BAPTISTERY OF SAN GIOVANNI

The Cathedral is located on the hill above the Campo so that Cathedral, Campo and market are all interrelated, an interrelationship that derives from their topographical location. Routes link the three spaces and the two routes from the Campo to the Cathedral each involve a gradual heightening of tension by occasional glimpses of the dome or campanile.

The most direct cathedral approach is through the main entrance to the Campo, along the street opposite, then climbing up stairs past the Baptistery and through an arch into the space beside the Cathedral. From this point the route traverses the southern side of the Cathedral in the square formed on this east-west axis, before turning towards the Cathedral entry point.

routes begin

arch

VIEW THROUGH ARCH

The second Cathedral approach is from either the Campo
entrance or the opening which gives a view enframing the
Torre del Mangia. This route passes first along the street
behind the Campo, then turning through a narrow alley
and climbing steeply towards an arch leading into the
space formed by the incomplete extension of the Cathedral.
On this route there are views of the Cathedral Dome and
campanile framed by the arch. Once alongside the
Cathedral the route continues along the main axes, this
movement being helped by the horizontal stripes on
the Cathedral.

CATHEDRAL

SIENA CATHEDRAL

The final act in the progression from the Campo is the magnificent west facade of the Duomo. As with the other symbols this facade fulfils a particular role. It speaks of entry to something of great importance, the Cathedral itself.

The facade forms part of a symbol system, which includes the Cathedral dome, the campanile, and the Torre del Mangia, these two towers relating to each other as if to cite their mutual interdependence.

These forms are part of a complex interrelated spatial and volumetric network in which Cathedral, Campo and market are each separately defined, and defined appropriately by significant configurations.

That they occur in a dense built-up city fabric only increases their potency and impact, and each space is created so as to allow the major buildings in them to be properly understood.

It is an organic arrangement in which site forces combine with practical needs to form spaces and to create built objects which symbolize special aspects of life. The symbolic hierarchy is clear, and becomes the more acceptable because it forms part of the bustling network of the city.

The major buildings act as symbols which identify those aspects of life seen as important by the Sienese in the Middle Ages. Supported by sculpture and paintings, the whole city becomes meaningful and rich in form and content, in every sense reflecting the lifestyle and concerns of people at a particular moment in time.

The evolution of the Piazza S. Marco is similar to that of the Cathedral/Campo complex in Siena in the way each ensemble organizes the architecture to reflect the history of each city and its social, political and religious values. In each case, a randomly disposed assemblage of dwellings is packed into the city fabric, compacted by defensive needs, satisfied at Siena by a fortified wall and at Venice by its isolation in the Lagoon.

In neither city were axial vistas possible, and any open space has to be carved out of the existing dense fabric; accordingly each piazza is in dramatic contrast to the city as a whole. Despite these similarities the cities are very different. Siena situated on a series of hills and routes in Tuscany, Venice, completely flat, surrounded by and in danger of being submerged by water. Influenced by its trading links with Byzantium, Venice has an ostentatious theatricality evidenced in the richness of its architecture and the splendour of its colouring. The city of canals is pervaded by reflective transparency, with blues, pinks, white and gold, in contrast to the brown and terra-cotta sobriety of Siena.

In contrast to the relatively anonymous architectural contributions in Siena, the power of Venice attracted the great names in architecture, painting and sculpture, with works by Carpaccio, Bellini, Giorgione, Titian, Canaletto, Veronese and Tiepolo, and buildings by Palladio, Sansovino Vignola and Scamozzi. The city comprises a fusion of the arts, reaching an architectural climax in the Piazza S. Marco, a dynamic juxtaposition of buildings and spaces that accord with the reality of needs over a period of time.

THE PIAZZA OF SAN MARCO, VENICE

SITE FORCES

WATER

The presence of so much water exerts a considerable force. To begin with there is a strong sense of continuous horizontality and during spring and summer the sparkling animation of the canals and blue Aegean sky charge the city with unusual effects of light and shade. The air of unreality provided by the setting is increased by symbolic connotations associated with islands. Originally the settlement was seen as a temporary refuge, an escape from the mainland, and islands inevitably suggest those romantic associations which often produce picturesque or exotic responses.

ROUTES AND VIEWS

The site is centrally located in relation to the entrance to the Grand Canal, with a direct route to the commercial area at the Rialto. The close proximity of the islands of S. Giorgio and Guidecca opposite give a sense of containment externally. There are views from the site towards these islands and towards the arrow-head point of the mouth of the Grand Canal. On approaching the site by boat the site affords sufficient frontage to be able to make a grand gesture similar to that in cities where space allows axial vistas, whilst internally there is sufficient containment for the creation of an enclosed 'private' domain. The potential for interaction between internal and external is exploited and refined by successive contributions over several centuries.

THE SITE

The site is surrounded on three sides by a labyrinth or 'maze' of buildings and routes. This mysterious disorder contrasts with the order and clarity of the piazza. The complex exploits the dramatic confrontation between these two opposing 'worlds'.

NORTH

RIALTO

PIAZZA

GRAND CANAL

SALUTE

the route to the Rialto
becomes a vista to S. Giorgio

BACINO

S. MARK'S CANAL

S. GIORGIO

S. GIORGIO MAGGIORE

GIUDECCA CANAL

GIUDECCA

The Piazza S. Marco is located at a convergence
of routes and acts as a focal point addressing
the city and the water.

131

ORIGINS

The first Piazza San Marco was formed in the space fronting the earlier Basilica. A campanile was begun in 888, but until the late twelfth century, a canal, just beyond the campanile, limited the size of the square. The fortress-like Doge's Palace is a reminder of the defensive origins of the city.

RIALTO

ROUTE TO RIALTO

VIEWS

ORIGINAL CHURCH

PIAZZA S. MARCO

BATARIO CANAL

CAMPANILE

PIAZZETTA

DOGES' PALACE

ORCHARD OF THE NUNS OF S. ZACCARIA

PLAN
(Based on a drawing in Piazza San Marco, Padua, 1970, p. 46)

NOTIONAL LAYOUT OF PIAZZA BEFORE 1173

Although far from complete, and unrecognizable as we now know the square, this embryonic state of the piazza contains the basic ingredients which do not change with time and which, when sensitively developed, ultimately ensure the success of the complex.

In essence these comprise nine important factors:

1) The establishment of the Basilica of St. Mark as the dominant mass with its main facade facing onto the piazza.

2) The combined linked masses of the centroidal Doge's Palace and Basilica on approximately the same orthogonal grid.

3) Containment of the north side of the piazza by a continuous plane at an oblique angle.

133

SITE FACTORS

4) The diminishing perspective effect caused by the oblique angles in both piazza and piazzetta.

PIAZZA

PIAZZETTA

5) The echelon lead-in to the piazza by the staggered alignment of the Basilica and Doge's Palace.

6) The location of the campanile at a centre of gravity and right angled pivot point in the ensemble.

4) The route/vista axis from the business district at the Rialto to the seat of government in St. Mark's Piazza.

8) Facades which face the Bacino

VIEWS

9) Twin facades on the Doge's Palace facing both Piazzetta and Bacino

135

ELEMENTS COMBINED

In 1173 Sebastiano Ziani, the Doge, bought the land containing the Batario canal, and a competition to organise the space was won by Nicolo Baraltiero who had built the giant granite columns at the end of the Piazzetta.

The canal was filled in in 1176 to almost double the size of the square and the church of S. Geminiano was moved back and rebuilt to form the western edge of the new paved piazza.

It was decided to have covered walks to enclose the piazza and houses and shops were arranged around the space, the houses being assigned to the nine Procuratori de Supra, officials who were in charge of St. Mark's and its properties. By the beginning of the fourteenth century, there was a covered walk all the way round the square, and during this period the Piazza S. Marco was the largest and best organized city square in Europe.

On the north side of the square, the first Procuratie, (built in the 12th century) had an arcade with 58 openings, making it a considerable medieval monument. which lasted 350 years.

The south and west sides of the Doge's Palace were finished by 1424. The 500' long Procuratie Vecchie was built between 1480 and 1517 by Bartolomeo Buon the Younger and Sansovino began his Library in 1536 to complete the Piazzetta. Sansovino also designed the Loggetta at the base of the Campanile.

The Clock Tower by Loducci was erected in 1499 and the three flagpoles with Leopardi's bronze bases were erected in 1505.

After Sansovino's death, Scamozzi finished the Library and built the Procuratie Nuove, begun in 1584, in the process detaching the Campanile and increasing the size of the square.

Under Napoleon, the church of S. Geminiano was pulled down enabling completion of the piazza on its west side.

CENTROIDAL MASS

In the final assemblage of elements, the site may be read as a flat platform with canals restricting the boundaries to the north, south and east

The Greek Cross plan of St. Mark's establishes a regular bi-laterally symmetrical form which has the inherent potential to dominate the space.

NORTH

EXOTIC DOMINANCE

This dominance is achieved by the projection of the church forward into the piazza and by the presence of five 'onion' domes which punctuate the skyline. A series of bold arched openings face the square, elaborately decorated, whilst the entire perimeter treatment combines with the domes to create a sculpted mass of great power and majestic richness. The arches, domes and general treatment give the mass a strong suggestion of verticality.

INTERLOCKING CONTRASTING MASSES

PIAZZA S. MARCO

movement axis between
buildings leading towards
stair giving access to upper
arcade in courtyard.

PIAZZETTA

MOLO

BACINO

The Doge's Palace is locked into the Basilica in
such a way that the two centroidal forms reinforce
each other and form a continuous solid mass.

The Basilica remains dominant, the courtyard erosion of
the Palace reducing its mass content. If St. Marks responds
to the Piazza, the Doge's Palace responds primarily to
the sparkling waters of the Bacino, yet it also faces the
Piazzetta in an echelon arrangement which guides movement
towards the Piazza.

Arcades enrich the Palace at the lower levels, giving the
upper mass a floating effect, and the insistent columnar
rhythm also guides movement from Molo to Piazza. If the
Basilica is earthbound with a vertical emphasis, the Palace is
horizontal and has a 'floating' sense of linearity despite
its centroidal configuration.

centroidal mass with domes

route and stair pin forms together.

centroidal mass with courtyard

CONTRASTING LINKED MASSES

The forms lock together to form a composite whole.

At the point of interlock a circulation route pierces the complex and rises by the scala dei Giganti to the second floor level of the inner cortile of the Doge's Palace.

A further route around the courtyard at ground level gives access to the Basilica. The network of circulation routes links Palace to Basilica and links both to the Molo and Piazzetta.

SCALA DEI GIGANTI

PIAZZETTA

MOLO

PLAN

SCALA DEI GIGANTI

CIRCULATION

MOVEMENT

LIBRARY OF ST. MARK

spatial curtain

VIEWS

The forward projection of Sansovino's Library turns movement into the Piazzetta. The colonnades of both Library and Doge's Palace direct this movement which is also assisted by the pattern of the floor paving.

The two columns at the end of the Piazzetta form an implied spatial curtain which helps to define the edge of the Piazzetta and also provides a frame for views outwards. The sense of framing is assisted by the diminishing perspective effect of the differing angles of the Library and Doge's Palace.

OBLIQUE PLANE

RIO DEL CAVALETTO

PROCURATIE VECCHIE

The combined dominant centroidal masses, St. Mark's Basilica and the Doge's Palace, establish an implied orthogonal field determined by their respective facades facing St. Marks' Piazza and the Piazzetta.

Restricted in its location and alignment by the Rio del Cavaletto at its rear, the Procuratie Vecchie fronts onto the north side of the piazza. Although in consequence a product of circumstances, the facade makes a dramatic oblique planar interaction with the orthogonal field which turns movement into the Piazza.

143

ENCLOSURE

St. Mark's Square is completed by the Procuratie Nuove on its southern side by Scamozzi, who completed the Library after Sansovino's death. Scamozzi's design of the Procuratie picks up the scale and rhythm of the Library but adds an extra floor to strengthen this side of the square.

The format is continued across the west side but is reduced to two storeys to match the height of the Procuratie Vecchie.

The sturdy centroidal mass of La Zecca (the Mint) by Sansovino provides a secure termination of the complex on the side facing the Bacino.

144

NEGATIVE SUPPORTING ENCLOSURE

POSITIVE DOMINANT MASSES

SPACE SPILLS OUT

CAMPANILE

The complete enclosure, with a more or less continuously regular roofline, contains the Piazza S. Marco and the western edge of the Piazzetta. The effect is of linear horizontality, these planes, with a strong rhythmic component, acting as a passive background to the main events which dominate and generate each space, the Basilica and Doge's Palace. This dual megastructure, with its echeloned alignment, fashions the positioning of the two spaces, with the Piazza spilling over into the Piazzetta at its south east corner.

The above plan of the piazza in about 1500 (taken from Lotz, 'Italienische Plätze') reveals the basic dilemma which is presented by the oblique alignment of the Procuratie Vecchie.

This stems from the way the oblique field so engendered, and which leads appropriately visually towards the Basilica, conflicts with the orthogonal field established by the Basilica and Doge's Palace. (Both fields are dotted in over the plan).

At this point in time, before Scamozzi's Procuratie Nuove, the Campanile is shown wedged into the southern side of the square.

PIAZZA

The positioning of the Campanile, detached by Scamozzi from the adjacent Procuratie Nuove, clearly defines and separates the Piazza from the Piazzetta. By breaking away the Campanile, the planar enclosure of both spaces is allowed to continue uninterrupted, giving a sense of continuity from Piazzetta to Piazza.

By its location, the Campanile helps to contain the Piazza and acts as an element framing the Basilica, which addresses the Piazza at an angle. Any doubt as to which field, orthogonal or oblique, should operate in the square, is resolved by the floor paving, which reinforces the oblique facade of the Procuratie Vecchie and directs the space, obliquely, towards St Mark's.

Scamozzi's alignment of the Procuratie Nuove, however, retains the orthogonal characteristic and the turn to the Library is a right angle. This orthogonal reading is not quite that of the Basilica and Doge's Palace; this axial shifting, sometimes slightly, sometimes boldly, is a major feature of the ensemble, animating the mass-space-planar relationships with a subtle dynamism.

The diminishing perspective induced by the angle of the Procuratie Vecchie exaggerates the apparent length of the square, this being enhanced by the close spacing of the hundred columns in the arcade.

space defined by flagpoles and Loggetta belongs to both Piazza and Piazzetta

PIAZZA SAN MARCO

LOGGETTA

CLOCK TOWER

PIAZZETTA

MOLO

The positioning of the Campanile also defines the Piazzetta as a linear space with its axis running approximately north/south. At the northern end the axis is concluded by the Clock Tower by Coducci, whilst to the south the axis runs through the easterly column which defines the edge of the Piazzetta as it meets the Molo. Further definition is provided by the three flagpoles fronting the Basilica. These flagpoles also entrame the Basilica as foreground incidents when St. Marks is viewed from the Piazza.

Sansovino's Loggetta, at the base of the Campanile, confirms the directional nature of the tower by ensuring that it faces the Piazzetta. This intervention, whilst retaining continuity of the axiality of the Piazzetta, further subdivides the space by creating a space fronting St. Mark's which belongs to both Piazza and Piazzetta.

The positioning of the Campanile also concludes the axis which pins the Basilica and Doge's Palace together and which leads to the Scala dei Giganti. The Campanile, therefore, whilst establishing the spatial definition of both Piazza and Piazzetta, forms part of the Basilica/Doge's Palace group and by its separation, does not belong to the planar enclosure around these spaces.

In its verticality, the Campanile relates directly to the vertical emphasis apparent in the Basilica, in this sense acting in contrast to the horizontal planar enclosure around the Piazza. Like both Basilica and Doge's Palace it is a major event, an object in the space and not simply an enclosing element. Placement of small windows to the left on each facade of the Campanile implies a sense of rotation, not inappropriate to its pivotal position and role.

MOVEMENT

PIAZZA S. MARCO

D

C

B ← A

MOLO

VIEWS FROM BACINO

VIEW A

VIEW B

VIEW C

VIEW D

VIEWS

The two most dramatic entry points into the Piazza occur as important routes emerge into the space at the south west corner and through the Clock Tower opening.

At the south west corner the view of St. Mark's and the Campanile is framed by an arch of the arcade surrounding the Piazza. Following movement through the 'maze' of narrow streets the drama and magnificence of this view is one of the finest in all architecture.

VIEW A

VIEW B FROM MERCERIA THROUGH CLOCK TOWER ARCH

VIEW A →

MOLO

view towards the Salute Church

view towards San Giorgio Maggiore.

After taking the route from the Rialto along the Merceria, the view through the arch of the Clock Tower is also a compelling visual event. Framed by the twin columns the axial vista leads towards San Giorgio Maggiore, focusing on Palladio's domed church. On reaching the Molo the view to the right is of the entrance to the Grand Canal and the Salute Church.

VIEW B

VIEW FROM CLOCK TOWER

INTERPRETATION

The Piazza S. Marco is an outstanding example of those qualities which ensure successful urban design. The reason for this has much to do with the way the role of architecture has been understood and fully expressed. Briefly stated, the Piazza addresses those issues of symbolism, pragmatism and the Genius Loci with which architecture is primarily concerned.

Successive contributions by gifted architects, selected by informed and responsible patronage, have produced an architectural masterpiece which operates on all levels demanded by the art. The time dimension has added to the totality in a manner that is entirely appropriate, because one of architecture's most important tasks is to represent both past and present aspects of a culture. This is particularly evident in the way each successive addition has respected the existing situation whilst managing to provide a positive and sensitive contribution.

That these additions have not always joined on to their neighbour immaculately (as with the corner junctions inside the Piazza) only adds to the vitality of the whole. Each architect has impressed his own personality on the ensemble and has been able to preserve the unity of the totality. The authority of the complex has much to do with the way each addition has responded to the specific conditions and requirements of its time.

If we consider the various buildings separately, each has considerable presence. The Basilica and Campanile are contrasting masses, each of which has a dominant role within the complex. There is a clear similarity with the Palazzo Pubblico and Torre del Mangia at Siena in the way these elements address both their respective piazzas and also signal the power and pride of their cities to distant horizons.

The Basilica expresses its Byzantine origins with an exotic imagery that celebrates both the power of the church and the vitality of the culture which it served. The exuberant majestic exterior contrasts with the mysterious solemnity of the interior, demonstrating that difference between light and darkness which must have coloured human experience in medieval times, when life was precarious and God so necessary.

If the Basilica speaks both of church and government, and is correctly dominant within the complex, the Doge's Palace fulfils another role, poised as it is, on the edge of both the Bacino and Piazzetta. The Palace has its Gothic vigour spiced with an Eastern ebullience which reflects and is reflected into, the sparkling blue waters which it faces. The Palace exemplifies the vitality of Gothic architecture, its inherent energy being fuelled by the powerful rhythm of its arcades, this animation being supported by the richness of its pattern and decoration.

Sansovino's Library is a perfect foil to the Palace, its elegance and sophistication contrasting with, yet complimentary to, the Gothic 'naivety' and extravagance of its neighbour. These buildings underscore the evolutionary advance in human consciousness from the Middle Ages to the Renaissance, yet, although separated by their respective world views, each design is strong and assured, the Library squat, compact, horizontal, with its own rhythms and rich decoration managing to be as powerful as its larger, elevated neighbour.

INTERPRETATION

Maintaining the Renaissance sobriety of the Library, the Piazza continues the Piazzetta theme of contrast between background and foreground. Whereas in the Piazzetta this is evident in the difference between Library and Doge's Palace, in the Piazza the enclosure is by buildings uniform in tone, containing the square as a receptacle for people and events, and above all for the Basilica. St Mark's provides the foreground, asserting itself not only by the richness of its three-dimensional form, but also by the way the evening sun adds visual warmth to the coloured mosaics facing the piazza.

Of especial importance in the Piazza is the obliquely angled Procuratie Vecchie. Not as rich sculpturally as the other two sides of the square, it has its own power, due partly to its oblique angle in relation to the other elements and partly to the insistent columnar rhythm of the arcade, these combined factors increasing the apparent length of the square.

The Clock Tower is appropriately picturesque in a Venetian sense. Whilst forming part of the Procuratie Vecchie, it cleverly stops the Procuratie rhythm and establishes an identity which expresses a dual function, that of clock and archway to a major route from the square. By raising the central section, containing clock and arch, the Tower concludes the axis leading through the Piazzetta to San Giorgio Compared to the Procuratie, of which it remains a part, the Clock Tower is light hearted, a delicate balance being struck between its playful figures and colouring and the dignity of the arcade alongside. This mixture of correct seriousness and an emotive theatricality, is also present in the relationship between the St Mark's/Doge's Palace group and the rest of the buildings in the complex.

Such juxtapositions give the complex humanity and ensure that it speaks to us on several levels, expressing a broad range of sensory experience. Sansovino's Loggetta has a 'weighting' which belies its size, acting as meeting point, viewing pavilion, termination of the axis towards the Scala dei Giganti, and also managing to turn the Campanile (otherwise directionally negative) towards the Piazzetta, and the two main buildings, Basilica and Doge's Palace.

The Piazza San Marco cannot adequately be discussed in stylistic or design terms but rather in terms of its extraordinary capacity and content. As with many great works of the human imagination, the ensemble balances formality and informality, unity and diversity, energy and control. We are presented with an architectural equation in which massing, surface treatment, movement progression and symbolic content fully engage the senses. To this must be added the magical time dimension which transports frail twentieth century man back to a glorious episode in his past.

In a description of Venice as seen through the eyes of the painter Giorgione, John Ruskin wrote:

"Have you ever thought what a world his eyes opened on... when he went down, yet so young, to the marble city — and became himself as a fiery heart to it?
A city of marble did I say? nay, rather a golden city paved with emeralds. For truly, every pinnacle and turret glanced and glowed, overlaid with gold or bossed with jasper... A wonderful piece of world. Rather itself a world... A world from which all ignoble care and petty thoughts were banished... No foulness nor tumult, in those tremulous streets... No weak walls could rise above them; no low-roofed cottage, nor straw-built shed. Only the strength as of rock, and the finished setting of stones most precious. And around them... still the soft moving of stainless waters... Above, free winds and fiery clouds raging at their will; — brightness out of the north, and balm from the south, and the stars of the evening and morning clear in the limit of arched heaven and circling sea."

J. Ruskin, The Stones of Venice, Vol 2 London 1896 p 183.

5
ANALYTICAL STUDIES
OF BUILDINGS

ALVAR AALTO TOWN HALL AT SAYNATSALO
1950-61

ALVAR AALTO

Of those architects considered to have been pioneers of modern architecture, the works of Frank Lloyd Wright and Alvar Aalto most closely correspond with the proposition advocated in part one of this book, that architecture results from an interaction between programmatic requirements, the Genius Loci and the culture in which the architecture exists.

To some extent this is true of Le Corbusier's work, but his belief in universal solutions leading to standardization and his artistic as opposed to 'building' approach to design, place his output outside the central concerns of Wright and Aalto, each of whom made a significant contribution to the domestic architecture within his own culture. In this, these architects can be compared with Lutyens, who in his early houses similarly proposed an architecture rooted in his native land and owing inspiration to both landscape and tradition.

However, with regard to the traditional architecture within their respective cultures, a major point of departure for both Wright and Aalto was the desire to establish a fresh approach to the manipulation of internal space, and especially to redefine the relationship between inner and outer space.

In the case of Wright and Aalto, these explorations resulted in what has been termed an organic architecture, in which the elemental organization responds to internal requirements and external conditions simultaneously, each architect seeking to lock his building into its immediate topography.

In so doing, each architect uses a different kind of geometry. In Wright's work the organization is often controlled by systems which ensure homogeneity and unity as a direct result of the geometry itself. This is evident in his use of axes, the pinwheel and interlock (see pages

Aalto's work, by comparison, is more relaxed, less geometrically deterministic and more malleable, concentrating particularly on how ensembles interact with the landscape. There is an inner as well as an outer 'fluidity' in the way elements merge into each other, corresponding closely to D'Arcy Wentworth Thompson's description of cell growth[1]. Aalto often gathers his elements around a central foyer or court[2] and uses radial configurations in combination with linear forms.[3]

[1] Discussing the form of any portion of matter Thompson describes this as a 'diagram of forces,' explaining how an Amoeba tends 'to be deformed by any pressure from outside.' He refers to the fluid state of the organism and how its shape responds to forces exerted upon it. D'Arcy Wentworth Thompson, On Growth and Form, Abridged Edition, ed. by T. Bonner, Cambridge University Press, Cambridge, 1961, pp. 11, 12.

[2] See page 84

[3] See page 62.

Church in Vuoksenniska (Imatra) 1956-59
(after an axonometric from Dizionario Enciclopedico di Architettura e Urbanistica, 1968-69.)

ITALY AND FINLAND

The town hall at Säynätsalo is one of Alvar Aalto's most representative works in that the small complex of brick and timber buildings around a court encapsulates several themes which developed during his career. These themes can be traced back to two powerful influences on him, the one resulting from a trip to Italy in 1924 when he visited Florence, Padua and Venice, the other being the pervasive effect of the landscape of his native Finland.

In 1926, explaining the importance to him of Italian hill towns Aalto had written: 'The town on the hill... is the purest, most individual and most natural form in urban design.'[1] The Italian hill town remained a source of inspiration throughout his life and became so interwoven with his perception of the Finnish landscape that he often read the latter in terms of the former: 'Central Finland frequently reminds one of Tuscany, the homeland of towns built on hills' and in a description of how villages in Finland could be transformed, he explains how when he sees these villages, in his mind's eye he would 'make the church stand out as a more dominating element among the houses by building a little colonnaded square in front of it or by raising its spire. (The open square surrounded by architecture, is one of the most powerful rhythmic accents available in hilly country).[2] In 1924 he wrote:

> Arriving at daybreak in a town which we have never been in before, we realize that there are laws, traditions, customs and details in this hustle and bustle which, just like the other phenomena of our day and age, are not just the movements of atoms, but energy directed into these channels and supervised by more developed individuals... Nothing does a town greater honour than a well-developed public life and beautiful, functional 'public places,' not the least of which is the market hall, the nerve center of its food distribution and morning bustle.[3]

[1] Quoted from Göran Schildt, Alvar Aalto, The Decisive Years, New York, 1986, p. 13.
[2] From Göran Schildt, Alvar Aalto, The Early Years, New York, 1984, p. 210.
[3] Ibid., p. 253.

Aalto had taken particular note of the vertical accentuation given by the campanile to the Italian hill town, and again applying the principle to his homeland wrote:

> Take an example, Ronnimäki Hill, which dominates the countryside around Jyväskylä, would only need a white campanile (tower) near (not at) the top for the whole area to acquire an extremely refined character. Even a lookout tower would do, but not one of those needlelike towers which function as a point of observation but not as an object of it. [1]

Despite the fact that the hillside on which the Säynätsalo town hall was sited had a very gentle slope which could not be compared to an Italian hill town, Aalto's design brings together several strands of his thoughts inspired by the visit to Italy. These include the notion of the town on a hill with the tower as a landmark, the enclosed court, the potential of stairs and the way architecture can mirror the vitality and express the essential character of a town.

[1] Ibid., p. 209.

SITE FORCES

↑ NORTH

TOWN HALL SITE

PROPOSED SITE PLAN   (not as built)

The main characteristics of the town hall site are:

1) The contours which delineate a gentle slope within a landscape of pine trees.
2) Two obliquely aligned routes which traverse the contours as they rise up the hill.
3) The layout of housing, echeloned alongside the routes but deployed rhythmically within the discipline of an orthogonal grid.

Typically Aalto's layout intended to reinforce the Genius Loci by strengthening linkages between routes, contours and the architecture. Responding to the setting of pine trees with their sense of randomness and verticality, Aalto proposes low horizontal buildings laid out in an informal yet ordered fashion.

The proliferation of trees on the hillside gives a strong sense of nature on the site. This is not, therefore, the typical urban site as would normally be the case for a town hall, but instead represents an unusually direct interaction between man's activities and nature.

The town hall is situated at a nodal point where the routes conjoin to form the town square.

A centroidal form is proposed for the town hall, so positioned as to terminate the echeloned blocks of housing which lead towards the node.[1]

The oblique route and its supporting echelon rhythm of housing together constitute a powerful external vector inducing pressure on the centroidal town hall.

[1] see Peter Eisenman, doctoral thesis, The Formal Basis of Modern Architecture, Cambridge University 1963 p. 150

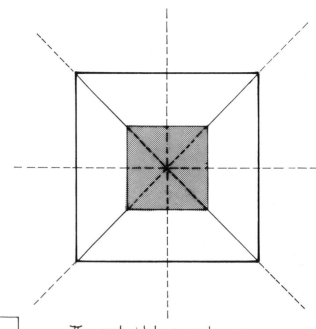

The generic form is centroidal, a symmetrical form with equal axes.

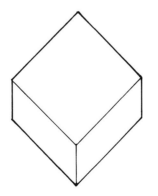

external vector

The centroidal mass becomes a courtyard. Sloping roofs point inwards to strengthen the feeling of enclosure. Echeloned housing produces an external vector which affects the form on the diagonal.

CONFIGURATIONAL READING

A symmetrical centralized mass eroded at its core or nucleus.

SYMBOLIC READING

A courtyard is a sheltered refuge which may suggest a sense of community. Diverse elements may be unified and become homogeneous around an enclosed courtyard.

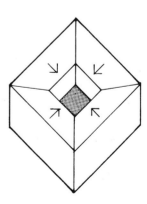

EFFECTS OF SLOPE

BACK

lateral axis

→   ←

Dominant facade   FRONT

The directionality of the slope changes the form so that the south facing facade assumes a dominant role. The form becomes directional.

The internal court is raised to provide two levels of accommodation.

On a slope the centre of gravity shifts to pull back the internal lateral axis.

lateral axis pulled back as centre of gravity shifts

NORTH   SOUTH

Inner court raised

SECTION

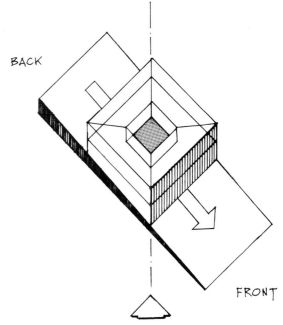

BACK

FRONT

CENTROID FRACTURED

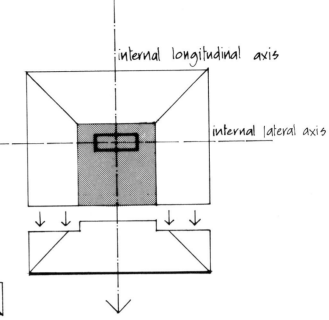

internal longitudinal axis

internal lateral axis

whole

internal lateral axis

part fractured

SECTIONS

[1] Eisenman argues that the library is sliced away from the court as a result of two lines of force, one from the east, the other from the south-west, these emanating from entry points at these corner junctions. Ibid., p. 152

The centroidal form is fractured by pulling away the southern side.[1]

A pool is placed within the courtyard where the internal axes meet. The form remains bi-laterally symmetrical and directional.

CONFIGURATIONAL READING
Fracture suggests possibility of tension between triple-sided court and separated part. Slightness of fracture retains gestalt of centralized mass with eroded nucleus.

SYMBOLIC READING
Courtyard enclosure and unity retained but court now accessible.

LIBRARY

SHOPS

SECTION

ACCOMMODATION

The upper level is concerned mainly with civic and public activities with shops on the lower floor to the south and east. Apartments are placed in the western block.

CIVIC

APARTMENTS

CIVIC

LIBRARY

Stairs give access to the court at the point of fracture. The south block is reduced in width but remains 'locked' into courtyard.

CONFIGURATIONAL READING

The form is bi-laterally symmetrical and the centralized mass with an eroded core remains as a gestalt. Where the southern block 'locks' into the court, the space at either side spills down in the form of stairs.

SYMBOLIC READING

Contact is established between the inner private world of the court and the exterior without diminishing the sense of shelter and privacy.

COUNCIL CHAMBER

SECTION
Council Chamber roof points in same southerly direction as does the fractured block.

possible location of council chamber as a visual stop to external vector

COUNCIL CHAMBER chamber located alongside entry.

secondary entry ▷   ◁ primary entry

The council chamber has a key role in the complex, partly due to its importance, but also because a large volume is needed to house its activities.

This allows the architect to provide a focus within the complex and also to provide a visual stop when seen from the approach route.

To do this, the chamber could have been placed on the oblique axis in the north east corner. Instead the chamber is located at the point of fracture, alongside the stair access from the public space. This relationship to the point of entry gives this particular entry added importance.

approach route direction

SYMBOLIC READING
As the main element, the Council Chamber dominates.

CONFIGURATIONAL READING
The bi-lateral symmetry is distorted.

external vector

SPIRALS

The council chamber acts as the pivot for two spiralling movements, both anti-clockwise, one ascending around the chamber, giving access en route, the other spiralling around the court as a glazed corridor which continues internally. [1]

Council Chamber and circulation echelon on oblique.

---

[1] Eisenman compares this spiral movement system to Le Corbusier's Pavillon Suisse, explaining the latter as the 'control of a pattern of behaviour, movement of people, which is external to the fabric of the building yet enforced on the observer by the presence of the building ... For Aalto the spiral movement is a quality of the work itself, the control of the volumetric arrangement by a perceptual reference to a generic spiral.' Ibid., p. 155.

SYMBOLIC READING

The spirals represent movement and in this case enclosure.

CONFIGURATIONAL READING

The Council Chamber pins one corner of the court. The courtyard spiral exerts pressure which threatens to close the south-western corner. An echelon on the west facade forms part of this pressure and the entire west side is strengthened to balance the mass of the council chamber. The council chamber entry point at court level extends out to form an enclosed corner of the court to the north-east. The pool is shifted off-axis towards this corner.

FLOW

The attempt to close the court at the south-west corner is prevented by a build-up of internal pressure within the court which flows out of the space in a cascade of steps on the diagonal.[1] This flow, like a powerful current, shapes its 'banks' so that the edge of the west block is cut back sharply. The sharpness of this fractured edge is complemented by a straight stair leading to the apartments in the west block. A projection and setback create a contained zone within the court.

[1] see Eisenman, Ibid., p. 154.

a chimney counterbalances the council chamber in a minor key.

projection strengthens corner

spiral

echelon

setback

projection strengthens corner

NATURE

Council chamber and library block act as stabilizing elements

PUBLIC AND CIVIC

PUBLIC AND CIVIC

southern block roof is distorted by acute fracturing at south-west.

NATURE

stair pulled towards external vector

oblique external vector

SYMBOLIC READING

The court may be interpreted either as a 'lake' which cascades outwards at its southern extremities, or more literally as a secluded garden with grass and planting. The contorted stair links the private world of the court with its landscape and symbolizes the organic energy inherent in Aalto's work. The stair, flowing on to the slope and into nature, contrasts with the regular formal stair leading from the public square to the civic realm of the council chamber.

CONFIGURATIONAL READING

The volumes which enclose the court are distorted by the pressures created. The southern block remains a stabilizing element linked to the council chamber.

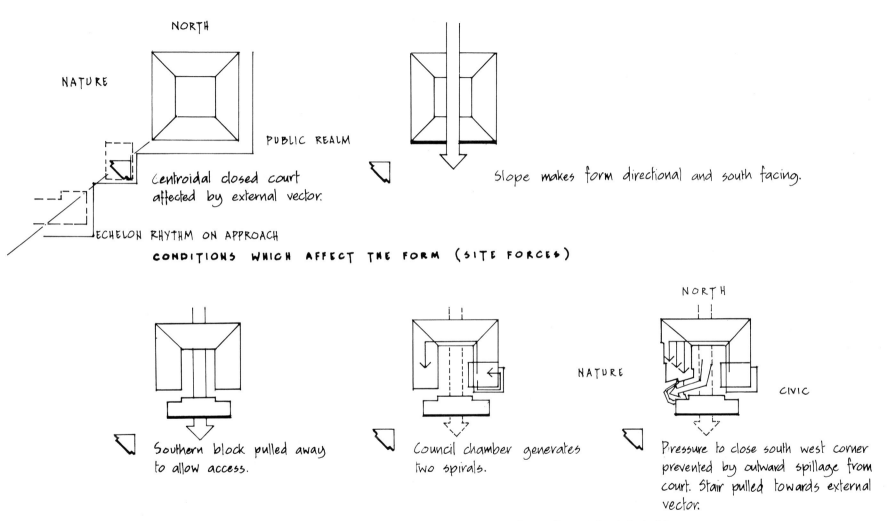

NORTH

NATURE

PUBLIC REALM

Centroidal closed court
affected by external vector.

ECHELON RHYTHM ON APPROACH

Slope makes form directional and south facing.

CONDITIONS WHICH AFFECT THE FORM (SITE FORCES)

Southern block pulled away
to allow access.

Council chamber generates
two spirals.

NORTH

NATURE

CIVIC

Pressure to close south west corner
prevented by outward spillage from
court. Stair pulled towards external
vector.

ORDERING OF THE FORM IN RESPONSE TO SITE AND PROGRAMME

There are similarities in the courtyard treatment at Säynätsalo and Le Corbusier's monastery at La Tourette (1957-60). For an analysis of the monastery see G. H. Baker, Le Corbusier: _An analysis of form_, (Second edition, 1989), Van Nostrand Reinhold (International) Co. Ltd., London, pp. 267-298.

DIAGONALS

As Eisenman points out,[1] the circulation corridor is fully glazed on two adjacent sides of the court, whereas the other two sides have windows placed in solid walling. This reaffirms the diagonal condition imposed by the external oblique vector.

The library is extensively glazed on its southern side, affirming the south-facing frontality of the complex.

Had this glazing faced the court the effect would be to destroy the internal court reading in terms of the external vector and would also have consolidated the introversion of the complex.

With the actual fenestration deployment, two site conditions are satisfied, 1) the effect of the oblique vector on the court, and 2) the south-facing frontality induced by the slope.

The diagonal condition within the court is part countered by the opposite diagonal generated by the council chamber echelon and terminated by the chimney.

[1] Ibid., p. 154.

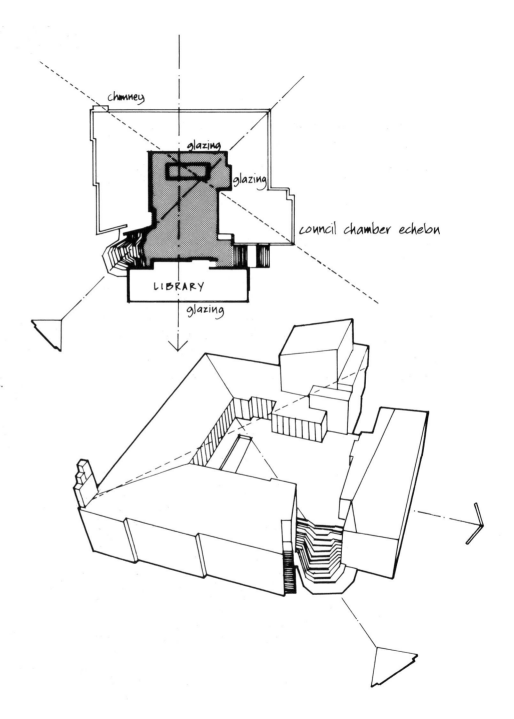

The council chamber and library act as stabilizing
elements which counter pressures within the court.
The lateral axis is developed in each configuration,
by an outward cantilever in the council block, and
by a linear deployment in the library.

The council chamber ensemble is locked on to
the library by a pergola which turns movement
into the civic suite. A brick paved area (visually
aligned with a projection from the library) is
placed alongside the pergola on a similar north-
south axis. This supports the locking effect of the
pergola and indicates a shift in the centre of
gravity towards the south east corner.

LIBRARY PLAN

echelon deployment along lateral axis of library

lateral axes developed by a series of vertical planes

COUNCIL CHAMBER

COUNCIL OFFICES

brick paving in circulation areas

wall stops and turns movement

brick surface helps to contain and define entry

ENTRY FOYER

reception counter on opposite diagonal to cantilevered stair above

COURTYARD LEVEL

COUNCIL CHAMBER

The main route into the Civic Suite ascends the formal stair, turning at right angles to enter beneath the pergola. The movement route is further turned by a wall which is the only solid element in the continuous glazing around two sides of the court. The reception counter in the foyer is echeloned on a diagonal which divides the space into public circulation on the courtyard side and office space and toilets opposite. The stair leading upwards towards the Council Chamber is opposite the circulation route which leads to offices around the court. Moving towards the Council Chamber the route spirals round, giving access at two different levels.

176

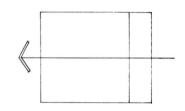

CUBIC BOX

DIRECTIONAL NORTH / SOUTH

CHAMBER ALIGNED EAST/WEST

REAR ADDITION

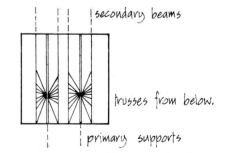

secondary beams

trusses from below.

truss in section

primary supports

CIRCULATION SPIRAL

ROOF SUPPORTED BY OUTSTRETCHED 'FINGERS'

174

ENERGY

FENESTRATION 'MOVES' AROUND CHAMBER

CANTILEVERS TO EAST

dominant facade

south facing planes
are mutually supportive.

The sense of energy around the Council Chamber is developed in several ways. The horizontal slit windows lighting the spiralling route highlight and reinforce the sensation of movement.

Lateral pressure to the east is developed by the double cantilever of the southern plane alongside the entry stairs.

The roof of the chamber dips down from south to north but also ascends again at each corner whilst taking a further dip on the northern side.

ROOF FALLS AND RISES IN 4 DIRECTIONS

Council Chamber and generic form each have orthogonal and diagonal characteristics of a square plan.

SYMBOLIC READING

At the heart of the ensemble and the community, the Council Chamber expresses its importance by its configurational arrangement. The plan is ordered and axial in an east/west direction. It is approached by a 'ceremonial' route after ascending the formal stair externally and the spiral route internally.

On the interior, the roof celebrates the aspirations of communal government with an emotive gesture in the form of the trusses, which speak of the trees and proud craftsmanship of the region.

The Chamber is the most expressive statement in the ensemble, representing order in its plan and energy in its three dimensional dynamism. The spiral movement symbolizes protection and heightens the importance of the Chamber itself.

Externally the upward tilt of the roof adds to the power and monumentality of the form. To the rear, the multidirectional pitches are similar to the roof trusses in evoking both the complexity and idealism of communal government.

CONFIGURATIONAL READING

The roof pitch gives the form a predominately south-facing role which conforms with a major characteristic of the complex. This alignment is reinforced by the power of the forward projection of the southernmost plane as it is extended by the spiralling route. This plane exerts pressure on the entry stair, whilst the cantilevers push the form out to the east, further strengthening the perceptual impact of the form.

To the rear of the roof, the corner treatment acknowledges the oblique characteristic of the complex. The spiral 'wrap-around' reiterates the orthogonal nature of the court and participates in the double spiral system generated by the chamber.

The chamber is therefore in a pivotal position, being pulled by two spirals, one around the court, the other around itself. The cubic form, with its roof rising (in different ways) to all four corners of the mass, is strong enough to resist any attempt to be pulled out of position by the spiral movement systems.

PERCEPTUAL FACTORS

Aalto's deployment of forms in the Säynätsalo Town Hall seems linked to his close examination of the Italian hill town. The complex offers a series of visual experiences concerned with discovery as movement from either approach into the complex is carefully controlled. The organization of the massing provides several messages, amongst which are suggestions of mystery, complexity, energy, monumentality, informality and repose.

Jeremy Blake has considered these issues in an analysis of perceptual factors in relation to each approach to the building.[1] Blake explains how the Council Chamber provides a visual incident when approaching from the west, with the opening leading to the raised court creating a desire to explore. Blake asserts that had the mass expressing the chamber been insignificant, the composition would have failed, particularly if the space had been allowed to leak out at the eastern entry point.

Blake goes on to illustrate how a larger mass would provide the necessary visual stop, but that this would remain unsatisfactory if the space could still leak out.

DRAWINGS AFTER J.M. BLAKE.
CAPTIONS BY J.M. BLAKE.

1 Jeremy M. Blake, 'Articulation, Alvar Aalto, Village Hall Säynätsalo,' Dissertation, School of Architecture, University of Newcastle-upon-Tyne, 1976

gap breaks sense of enclosure

mass not emphatic

1) **APPROACH FROM THE WEST**
DESIRE TO ENTER AND EXPLORE, BUT WEAKNESSES IN COMPOSITION WITH SIZE OF DISTANT MASS AND GAP WITH VIEW OUT BREAKING SENSE OF ENCLOSURE.

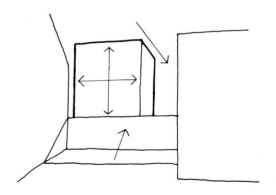

2) INTRODUCTION OF LARGE MASS ASSERTS SENSE OF FULL STOP ALTHOUGH WEAKNESS STILL EXISTS WITH VIEW OUT. RELATIONSHIP OF MASSES MORE EQUAL AND STATIC. PERMANENCE AND CALM.

WEAK CORNER →

3) VITALITY AND DRAMA BY CONTRASTS IN DIRECTION
OF PITCHES AND OBLIQUE APPROACH UP STEPS.
DOMINANT FACADE WEAKENED BY VIEW LEAKING OUT
AND BY ANGLE OF VISION.

4) FURTHER VITALITY BY STEPPING OF SIDE MASSES.
SENSE OF ENCLOSURE WITH MYSTERY OF PARTS UNSEEN.
UPWARD ENTRY REINFORCED BY STAIRS TO APARTMENT.
WEAK CORNER OF COUNCIL CHAMBER STRENGTHENED.

5) COUNCIL CHAMBER ROOF DIRECTIONS STABILISE THE MASS
YET MAINTAIN EMPHASIS ON FRONT FACADE. THE EYE IS
LED TOWARDS ENTRANCE UNDER PERGOLA AS WELL
AS TOWARDS WHAT IS OUT OF SIGHT IN RAISED
COURTYARD. THERE IS A COMPLETE FUSION WITH THE
SITE BY THE IRREGULAR FLIGHT OF GRASS COVERED
STAIRS. THE MASSES ARE RESTRAINED AND DOMESTIC YET
THEY MAINTAIN A SENSE OF VITALITY AND MONUMENTALITY.

CONCEALMENT AND MYSTERY

WEAK CORNER

1) **APPROACH FROM THE EAST**
MYSTERY OF EXPOSED YET ENCLOSED SPACE
HEIGHTENED BY RAISED CENTRAL AREA. DESIRE
TO ENTER AND EXPLORE.

3) THE ROOF PITCH OF THE COUNCIL CHAMBER CREATES
ASSERTIVE AND DIRECTIONAL 'FRONT' FACADE.
HOWEVER LOWER POINT OF MAIN MASS SEEMS WEAK
AND FORM REMAINS SIMPLISTIC.

2) LARGER BUILDING MASS INCREASES DRAMA OF
CONTRASTS IN THINGS SEEN AND NOT SEEN.
APPROACH INTO RAISED COURTYARD MADE MORE
MONUMENTAL AND MYSTERIOUS. NO SENSE OF
FRONT OR REAR.

4) SENSE OF MYSTERY CONFIRMED BY PERGOLA WHICH
ACTS AS GATEWAY TO UNSEEN UPPER LEVEL.
MONUMENTALITY OF MASS MAINTAINED BUT CENTRAL
ELEMENT BROKEN DOWN TO INDUCE SCALE AND
VITALITY. CONTRAST BETWEEN OBLIQUE UPWARD
ENTRY AND OUTWARD PULL OF COUNCIL CHAMBER
CIRCULATION. COLUMN EMPHASIZES RELATIONSHIP
WITH GROUND. WEAK CORNER OF COUNCIL CHAMBER
ROOF STRENGTHENED. FENESTRATION IN SOUTHERN
(LIBRARY) BLOCK TURNS CORNER AND POINTS
TOWARDS ENTRY STAIR.

5) FROM THE CIVIC SQUARE THE ASSERTIVE RHYTHMIC
SLATTED FACADE DOMINATES. BUT THE MASSING
OF THE COMPLEX DRAWS THE EYE BEYOND —
TO THE LEFT THE UNSEEN BECKONS AS THE
CONVOLUTED STAIR INDICATES ENTRY, WHILST
THE TWO LOWER PARTS OF THE SLATTED WINDOW
MULLIONS DRAW THE EYE TO THE RIGHT. IN
THIS DIRECTION THE CHAMBER AWAITS DISCOVERY.

BOLD AND DEFIANT

CIVIC APPROACH UP A GRANITE STAIR. FACADES BOLD
AND ALMOST DEFIANT YET RESTRAINED BY SCALE
OF WINDOWS AND PROJECTIONS. SENSE OF PERMANENCE
AND CALM AS WELL AS MYSTERY AND AUSTERITY.

Blake's analysis of movement towards the building underscores the way Aalto uses massing to control the visitor. On approaching, the courtyard, with its detached southern block, suggests something beyond, an idea confirmed by the visually evident Council Chamber.

Aalto's forms are arranged so as to draw the visitor forward in ways that are appropriate to each approach route and his surface treatment locks the complex into the site in a manner that is specific to every part of the building.

Aalto also deals with the emotional responses of the observer, and as Blake points out, the complex manages simultaneously to suggest monumentality, a degree of domesticity, permanence, calm and vitality.

Aalto's design approach deals with the programme, the Genius Loci and meaning. His use of brick and timber has a cultural reference in that these materials are widely used in Finland. In its form, the building expresses the life of the community, and its relationship to the setting speaks of the strong sense of the landscape that pervades this country of forests and water.

Aalto's lighting philosophy takes account of specific needs within the complex and the way fenestration affects surface treatment and massing.

In the Council Chamber a large window lets in light from the north, whilst an echeloned window admits western sun. On the periphery, strip windows at high level light the circulation route which moves around the edges of the chamber.

The large northern window is placed centrally on the wall surface, giving a sense of symmetrical stability to a facade with a roof which pitches sharply upwards. As this is the rear of the mass, the erosion of wall surface caused by such a large window is appropriate, allowing the main weighting to be at the south-facing dominant side of the configuration. This northern plane is a clear stop to the modelling around the chamber, which builds outwards to the east and south, the spiral of the route being clearly indicated by the 'ribbon' of glazing.

The small echeloned window to the west filters the light so that the low rays of the western sun do not shine directly into the chamber. Its surface location does not erode the mass, which retains its power on the courtyard side, and its size gives scale to the facade.

REAR PLANE PROVIDES STOP TO MODELLING

REAR FACADE SECONDARY

SYMMETRICAL WINDOW GIVES STABILITY

DOMINANT FACADE

COLUMN PARTICIPATES IN CORNER EMPHASIS.

ECHELON WINDOW AT DIP IN ROOF PROFILE.
SIZE AND LOCATION GIVES SCALE.
SERIES OF VERTICAL RHYTHMS LINK ROOF,
COURTYARD GLAZING, PERGOLA AND CIRCULATION
AROUND COUNCIL CHAMBER.

TILED PLINTH TO COURT

VERTICAL MEMBERS GIVE SUBTLE LINK BETWEEN
COURTYARD GLAZING RHYTHM AND PERGOLA.

RICHARD MEIER
THE ATHENEUM NEW HARMONY 1975-79

RICHARD MEIER

If Säynätsalo is a consummate demonstration of Aalto's organic architecture, Richard Meier's Atheneum at New Harmony, Indiana, similarly encapsulates the salient characteristics of the architect's personal style.

As Kenneth Frampton has explained,[1] Meier's work falls into an American tradition following on from the work of such influential Europeans as Mies van de Rohe and Walter Gropius. Frampton points out that a 'third generation' of American architects have developed a style relating 'more to the Romantic end' of the American 'ideological spectrum than to the Neoclassical ethos stemming from Mies.'

This third generation, continuing 'the tradition of the International Style through its independent return to pioneer sources,' comprised a group of three, Peter Eisenman, Michael Graves and Richard Meier. Later the group extended to John Hejduk and Charles Gwathmey.

Eisenman, Graves and Meier[2] were originally influenced by Colin Rowe, particularly by his interpretations of Le Corbusier's villas of the late twenties, and if Graves has shifted his position significantly away from these models, a modified Corbusian influence still pervades the work of Richard Meier.

[1] K. Frampton, Introduction to Richard Meier Architect, Buildings and Projects 1966-76, New York, 1976, p 7.
[2] Ibid., p. 8.

Typical of Meier's early work, the Smith House at Darien, Connecticut, although built in timber, has a distinctly Corbusian flavour in its compact organization, abstract imagery and sculptural presence. The house also demonstrates central principles of Meier's design strategy in the clarity and rigour apparent in his diagrammatic categorization of programme, structure, circulation, enclosure and entrance.

However, if a direct comparison be made between the Smith House and two of Le Corbusier's more canonical works, the Villa Savoye and 'Les Terraces', (the Villa Stein de Monzie at Vaucresson) the differences are as important as the similarities.[3]

Le Corbusier's villas, although fully exploring the interaction between volume and space, using transparency and erosion of the mass as means of extending contact between the villas and their landscape, are characterized by three distinct 'restrictions.'[3] First, the use of concrete establishes its own kind of plasticity resulting in a strong sense of mass; second, Le Corbusier's adherence to the Greek classical tradition gives him a greater reliance on axiality as a discipline, resulting in his work having an inevitable monumentality; third, Le Corbusier's villas (including the Jaoul Houses) have a strong sense of horizontal stratification. By comparison, the Smith House is more

[3] See my analyses of Le Corbusier's villas in Le Corbusier: An analysis of form. (Third Edition 1996) E. and F.N. Spon, London.

189

THE SMITH HOUSE

relaxed, more concerned with planes rather than mass and has a vertical rather than horizontal reading. The house evokes images of the American domestic tradition of Richard Neutra in particular, whose expansive and glamorous houses suggested an openness and opulence that is American and not European. Although as compact as Le Corbusier's villas, the Smith House is more permeable, but in its elaborate interplay of mass and membrane the house has a Corbusian richness of articulation.

These characteristics are retained in other important works, notably in the House at Old Westbury, so strongly reminiscent of the International Style, and in the Douglas House, which extends ideas generated in the Smith House.

Meier's plastic virtuosity and the capacity of his architectural language is demonstrated throughout his work, and the Atheneum, presenting a different kind of opportunity as a public building, has, like Le Corbusier's artist's residences, the right ingredients for Meier in being a very special kind of commemorative museum/information centre. This special quality emerges from the nature of the programme, with its historical and ideological associations, and the site, these enabling Meier to exploit an articulation system based on circulation and an orthogonal grid to form a typically complex and elaborate statement.

THE SMITH HOUSE
DARIAN CONNECTICUT 1965-67

The town of New Harmony was founded by George Rapp and his followers in 1818. The Harmonists, as they were called, came from Wurttenburg in Germany. They were intensely religious, industrious, and believed it was necessary to create a harmonious world to prepare for Christ's second coming.

This religious community was self-sufficient and was based on agriculture and the making and selling of goods and merchandise. They lived communally, so everything could be shared — no rich, no poor, everyone to be equal.

In spite of its prosperity, there were problems, and so in 1825 New Harmony was sold to the Scottish philanthropist, Robert Owen. He sought to further those ideals on which his utopian community of New Lanark in Scotland had been based. Owen, like Rapp, was committed to the idea of a model community and attracted a wide following of scientists and educators.

This rich heritage and commitment to religion, science and education, powerful and universal utopian ideals, provided the roots for a community that embodied the spirit of energy and those heroic visions on which America was founded.

These idealistic beginnings to the town of New Harmony have continued through the nineteenth and into the twentieth century and it is presently enjoying a renaissance based on tourism. This influx of visitors has given cause to restore the historic buildings as reminders of the town's cultural heritage, but also to build a centre-piece — the Atheneum — for its historic district.

This tourist information centre at once expresses the modernity of the twentieth century, but also contains subtle clues to the past and has a pivotal role in the understanding of the town's complex history.

The architect, Richard Meier, was asked to conceive a building as a place in which the public would become aware of the uniqueness of this historic town. He was asked to provide a building which would use modern materials and techniques and which would give visitors a sense of excitement as they arrive at the town.

SITE FORCES

The Atheneum site is at a point where the river and the town interact with each other; the site is at the edge of the town, between it and the river. Because the river floods to varying levels each year, the site is raised on a shallow plateau. From this elevated location, views are in an arc around the site with good views towards the river and the town.

The river surges at an angle to the town, this being apparent in the way the bridge bends to cross the river, its angle being at variance with the town grid.

The placement of the Atheneum on the edge of the town by the river is appropriate because this way the town is preserved intact and the building can express those intellectual ideals on which the town was founded in an entirely modern way.

These two forces, town and river, are quite different. The river is broad, a powerful surging force bordered by trees and cornfields. It is visually compelling and the best views are towards it.

ORTHOGONAL GRID OF NEW HARMONY

CORNFIELD

TREES

BEST VIEWS

RAISED PLATEAU OF SITE

POWERFUL SURGE OF WABASH RIVER

THRUSTING LINEAR FORCE OF BRIDGE

N

SITE PLAN

3 ZONE WHERE SITE MEETS TOWN

4 CORNFIELD ZONE

1 APPROACH ZONE

CONFRONTATION

2 RIVER ZONE

ZONES

By contrast, the town is a more placid ordered affair. It has a regular grid and is a product of man's imagination. So the task of the building is to mediate between man, as expressed through his intellectual idealism and the powerful and beautiful forces of nature.

The way the bridge crosses the river at an angle seems to symbolize this interaction between man and nature. If we think of the site as a series of zones, there are four of these. First there is the zone of approach from the town. Most visitors arrive along the road forming the central axis of New Harmony, then turn at right angles towards the building. Secondly there is the zone between the building and the river, this being a symbolic access route from the river. Third there is the zone where the site meets the town, and fourth there is the area to the northeast, a cornfield surrounded by trees. Giving priorities to these zones, the approach is most important because this is the first point of contact, of confrontation, between visitor and building. Second is the river zone, where the building relates to the river and takes advantage of the views. Third is the zone where site and town meet, and fourth, the cornfield zone to the north and northeast.

ORTHOGONAL GRID

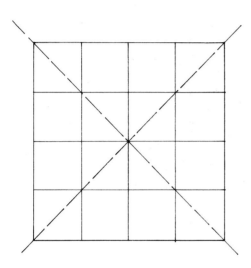

GENERIC SQUARE

Given the site conditions, Richard Meier exploits the opportunities by placing a square box on the site plateau with a structural grid adhering to that of the town grid. It is regular, symmetrical and orthogonal.

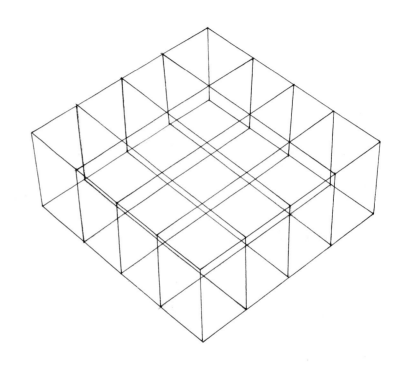

REGULAR SYMMETRICAL ORTHOGONAL

FUNCTIONAL GRID

FOUR ZONES

The regularity of the orthogonal grid changes to
accommodate internal functional needs resulting
in a changed module. The new grid system can
be subdivided into four distinct zones.

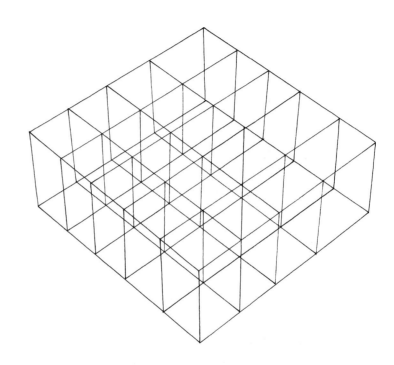

ADJUSTMENT TO ORTHOGONAL GRID

VISUAL RANGE

AUDITORIUM

MAIN VISUAL RANGE

Accepting the prime visual opportunities as extending in an arc from north to southeast, Meier places the closed box of the auditorium on the northeastern side of the site.

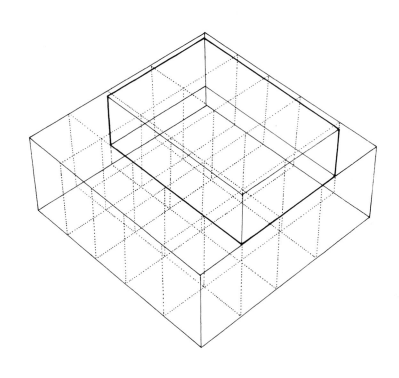

The way the auditorium is placed reorganizes the zones within the grid, resulting in the formation of two zones within the box, one larger than the other, a primary zone facing the river and a secondary zone facing the approach route.

RAMP

AUDITORIUM

A ramp is placed adjacent to the auditorium so that it reinforces the linearity of the primary zone.

A 5° angle is introduced to the design so that the ramp adjusts to the new alignment. A core is formed where the two grids meet.

ROUTES

This new grid extends at right angles
to form two routes, one from the river,
the other from the town.

TO RIVER

TO TOWN

RAMPED STAIR RISES TO SECOND LEVEL

200

STAIR AND SCREEN

The new grid emerges from the box to form a stair to the north and a screen to the south. The stair ends the linear thrust taking it down to the ground like a lightning conductor, and it belongs to both grids. The route out of and into the building from the town punctures the screen and the screen emerges from the form as a thrusting linear force with horizontal components which define the floors.

TO RIVER

Meier has explained the genesis of the slight shift in grids as being connected with the difference in the skewed edge of the river bank and the orientation of the town grid.

TO TOWN

201

SQUARE OVERLAY

A more radical rotation of a slightly larger square is placed across the first, tilting the form even further. Within these rotational forces the original grid and auditorium act as stabilizing elements.

SCREEN AND STAIR

A screen delineates the square to the southwest giving expression to the turning moment. The corner is stated by the horizontal edge to an observation deck so that the vertical screen and horizontal edge come together to form a thrusting axis pointing along the original grid towards the river.

At the opposite corner a square staircase has its own turning momentum, again taking a route downwards in a cascading motion to meet the route leading out of the building.

OBSERVATION DECK AT SECOND LEVEL

203

APPROACH

The rotated square forming the screen provides a planar barrier, which upon arrival to the building turns the eye towards the river.

On approaching from the parking area, the eye and movement is turned towards the river. The approach route is at 90° to the screen, which prevents any view into the building.

The screen is cut away to allow the insertion of an entry box. The large scale of the screen is used to attract the eye towards the entry box, this having human scale.

The entry box is aligned with the auditorium and is just off the movement axis on the route towards the building from the river. It provides a visual focus as the visitor moves towards the building, either from the river or from the car park.

HOVERING PLANES

Just above entry, a triangular gallery is placed so that the floor plane is above that of the adjacent observation deck. These horizontal planes meet at the corner, giving two sharp edges to reinforce the sharp edge of the vertical planar screen. This corner of the building resembles the prow of a ship and thus reinforces the prevailing shipboard imagery of the whole composition.

GALLERY

SECOND LEVEL PLAN

DYNAMIC CORNER

A further triangular plane hovers above as part of a roof observation deck. This locks back onto the vertical plane as part of a dynamic juxtaposition of planes at entry.

OBSERVATION DECK AT THIRD LEVEL

CURVED GALLERY

Adjacent to this vigorous clashing of planes, a curved box hovers above ground level, its wavy form responding to the river. This box provides a contained viewing gallery, its curved ribbon window framing views of the river. The serene curved solidity of the box contrasts with the animated series of planes alongside.

VIEWS TOWARDS RIVER

VIEWING DECK

VIEWING GALLERY BELOW

THIRD LEVEL PLAN

Between the curved viewing box and triangular gallery, the observation deck forms one side of a light well into the building so that light penetrates down into the sides of this space and also into the central circulation space formed by the ramp. A stair links the deck level with the gallery.

GALLERY

SECOND LEVEL PLAN

WEST FACADE

STAIR | VIEWING GALLERY | PLANES | SCREEN

VIEWING GALLERY

W E S T   F A C A D E

Visual movement along the west facade is from right to left, stopping at the stair, which forms a vigorous zigzag, taking the eye down to the ground.

The composition integrates four major elements: the screen, which is a vertical plane; the hovering horizontal planes; the curved viewing box and the stair. The entry box also provides an important visual incident.

The stair pierces the viewing gallery at its northern end where the gallery extends to give access to the auditorium.

On the south side of the building, a
screen is placed on the main grid. This
is joined back to the auditorium in the
form of a projection box at high
level. Below this, the screen is open
except for slender vertical supports
and horizontal ties back into the main
structure.

AUDITORIUM

GALLERY

The route from the building at gallery
level continues to the ramp, the railings
intensifying the linear force of the route.
The angle of the ramp continues to form
the inclined angle of the screen. It is
as if the ramp could be pushed back
into the screen.

PENETRATION TO SOUTH

At an **upper** level, a conference room forms a space leading across a bridge to an observation deck. This is situated on the roof of the curved observation box. From the conference room, a stair descends onto the route out of the building, sliding alongside the main linear route in support of it.

PENETRATION THROUGH
GLAZED MEMBRANE
ANGLED SCREEN SEPARATES
TWO DISTINCT ZONES

OBSERVATION
DECK

CONFERENCE
ROOM

SCREEN ACTS AS
VISUAL BARRIER

LIGHT PENETRATES FROM
ABOVE TO GALLERY BELOW

ROUTE TOWARDS THE TOWN

SENSE OF PENETRATION FROM SOUTH
INDUCED BY EROSION OF SCREEN
AT LOWER LEVELS. THIS MAKES
VISIBLE LINEAR HORIZONTAL PENETRATION
BY ROUTE AND VISUAL PENETRATION
THROUGH LARGE GLAZED AREAS

Where the stair emerges from the conference room and meets the lower route, two solid panels punctuate the railings, indicating these pauses on the route. Apart from the auditorium and its projection box, this south side is mainly glazed, giving a sense of its penetrability. Unlike the west side, there is a distinct feeling of contact to the south, contact between building and town, the route leading towards the town.

212

SOLID UPPER PLANE OF SCREEN IMPLIES A PLANE BELOW
THIS IMPLIED PLANE IS DEFINED BY COLUMNS AND FORMS
A SPATIAL 'CURTAIN'

HORIZONTAL PULL OF
EXTENDED SCREEN

ROUTE PASSES THROUGH IMPLIED AND ACTUAL PLANES

PUNCTUATION POINTS AT TOP AND BOTTOM OF STAIR TO CONFERENCE
ROOM SLOW DOWN THE MOVEMENT AS THE BUILDING IS ENTERED

PROJECTION BOX CONTAINS ROUTE, GIVING A TUNNEL-LIKE EFFECT AS
ROUTE PASSES UNDER
SCREEN GIVES SENSE OF
CONTAINMENT

PERSPECTIVAL EFFECT AS ROUTE PASSES THROUGH FRAME
ROUTE ENTERS GALLERY, IN SO DOING PUNCHING THROUGH THE ANGLED PLANE

STAIR DIRECTS THE EYE
TOWARDS ROUTE AND TOWN

VIGOROUS TWISTING
OF STAIR INCREASES
DYNAMISM AS ROUTE
ENTERS FRAMING

The route to and from the building is framed by
vertical and horizontal beams. The route passes
through implied and actual planes, sliding behind
the outer screen and thrusting through the planes.
The framing contributes towards a perspectival
effect along the route.

TRANSFORMATION OF BOX

CUBIC BOX

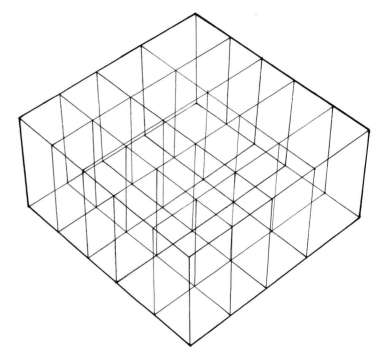

ORTHOGONAL GRID

If we summarize the development of the analysis, the initial box dissolves into planes and solids about two grids. Then along the new grid Meier pushes his linear route through, emerging from the building in the form of a ramp. Finally, a square is imposed on the cubic form allowing the formation of the front screen and square stair.

PLANES AND SOLIDS

STAIR AND CORE ON BOTH GRIDS

SOLID CORE

SOLID AUDITORIUM AND
PROJECTION BOX

PLANAR
SCREEN

VIEWS FROM CURVED BOX

FLOORS AS HORIZONTAL PLANES

CONTACT THROUGH FRAME

ENTRY BOX

PLANAR SCREEN

TILTED AXIS

PLANES AND SOLIDS ON TWO GRIDS

SQUARE IMPOSED

ROUTE ON TILTED GRID

RAMP 'SLIDES' INTO SCREEN AND
ROUTE PUNCHES THROUGH TILTED PLANE

SQUARE STAIR

ROUTE LEADS TO TOWN

LIGHT PENETRATES THROUGH 'WELL'

FLOOR PLANES MODELLED
TO OBLIQUE SCREEN

ENTRY BOX BECOMES VISUAL FOCUS

SCREEN ACTS AS BARRIER

LINEAR ROUTE

ROUTE CONTINUES TOWARDS RIVER

SQUARE IMPOSED

216

CURVED ADDITION

To complete the form, an addition is placed on the rear of the building. It is curved in response to the natural setting, the soft pastoral quality of the cornfield.

This is added onto the cubic mass, and the angle of the extremity is determined by the stair which is on the second grid. This addition locks the stair into the whole.

A square window concludes the composition and makes a very strong design statement. This square punctuation seems to emphasize the solidity of the mass to the rear. As with the two sets of stairs and oblique screen on the approach route, the window draws attention to one of the corners by pulling the eye toward it. This window lights the auditorium and forms part of a movement sequence inside. The support for the overhang also contains the boiler flue.

VISUAL INCIDENTS DRAW THE EYE TOWARDS EACH CORNER

VIEW FROM NORTH EAST

ANGLE OF ADDITION DETERMINED BY SECOND GRID AT 5° TILT

A comparison can be made between Meier's north elevation and the east facade of Le Corbusier's Chapel at Ronchamp.[1] In each case the upper volume forms a spatial 'curtain' which can be likened to the proscenium arch in a theatre.

1 see G.H. Baker, Le Corbusier: An analysis of form, (Third Edition, 1996) E. and F.N. Spon, London. p. 256

THE EYE IS LED PAST THE CURVE, BELOW IT, AS THE LOWER VOLUME IS CUT AWAY. THE STAIR TO THE WEST STOPS THE SPACE AT THE RIVER SIDE WHILST THE TURNED SQUARE STAIR DIVERTS THE EYE TOWARDS THE RAMP.

GROUND LEVEL

GLAZED MEMBRANE
RELIEVES COMPRESSION

COMPRESSED HORIZONTALITY

RECTILINEAR VISUAL FIELD
GIVES SERENITY AT CENTRE OF GRAVITY

ASCENT BEGINS

GLAZED EDGE GIVES CONTACT

STRETCHED SECONDARY GRID

218

On entry, the eye is drawn to the information counter. The space to the left of entry is kept low with a feeling of compression which begins on movement through the entry box. The low scale is preserved by the entry desk whose high counter top has the effect of making the ceiling seem lower. The sense of horizontal compression is relieved by the glazed curved membrane at the edge of the space and by a higher ceiling to the right of entry in the triangular section.

Two low bench seats reinforce the feeling of compressed horizontality between the floor and ceiling. Being directly opposite each other, they form a rectilinear visual field which has a stabilizing role, being at the centre of gravity in the composition. The serenity which they provide helps to prepare for the vigorous animation of the movement sequence.

From the information counter, movement is under the ramp projection above and adjacent to the base of the ramp. The ramp, which leads to the floor above the main entry space, draws the eye by its sculptural form. The ramp reinforces the feeling of stretching imposed by the second grid and sets in motion the spatial sequence from the low horizontal entry space in a gradual ascent through a central vertical shaft which is toplit above the ramp. The space is stretched out along the oblique plane of the secondary grid. The core and counter observe this grid as does the final ascent of the ramp and eastern side of the external stair.

The orthogonal grid is stated by the way the columns are disposed and the overlaid square is expressed through the screen adjacent to entry. The space is animated by the tension between the primary grid and the stretched secondary grid.

SECOND LEVEL

At the second level, the spatial compression is reversed with the low ceiling to the triangular gallery now behind the screen. The gallery to the curved viewing box, being at a lower level, has a higher ceiling. Between the two is the light well.

The visual dynamism consists of the combined interaction of spiraling stair and the swirling outer wall of the viewing box (supported by the swirling curved container for exhibits) these being set against the stretched angled wall into which the triangular gallery adds further dynamism. As on the entry level, triangle and curved box are set against each other dramatically.

Behind the stretched, angled, wall the triangular gallery contains the model of New Harmony. This has a curved end which becomes part of the ceiling above. Light is fed down in the gap between the cutaway and the external oblique screen.

CONFERENCE
ROOM

At the third level, the curvilinear counterpoint continues
with the conference room also having a cutaway
floor and ceiling.

As with the viewing box, exhibit cases reinforce
the spatial modelling in the conference room. A
rectilinear case contrasts with the part curved
case at the cutaway edge. The conference room
furniture, also designed by Meier, picks up the
major theme of the building's composition in
its precise expression of structure and form.

LIGHT DESCENDS
BEHIND SCREEN

The cascade around the core descends on the first orthogonal grid turning at right angles at the narrow end of the core. This right-angled turn is echoed above by the flat top to the core and secondary wall containing the uppermost viewing deck. These walls, at right angles to each other, have one side on the first grid and one side on the second. This interplay of cascade and dual grids (with an implied sense of rotation) is the most elaborate three-dimensional construct within the ensemble.

VISUAL INTERLOCK

The climax in the three-dimensional modelling of these elements occurs in the way Meier crashes together the curved viewing box and the cutaway layers in the triangular section behind the screen.

They slot together about the light well, which is also part of the exciting cascade of rooflights and the corkscrew of the spiral stair.

Vertical space, cascading glass, sloping ramp and hovering planes are all locked together in a way that is determined by the function of each element.

ELEMENTS LOCK TOGETHER ABOUT THE LIGHT WELL FULLY EXPLOITING THE DUAL GRID SYSTEM

MOVEMENT SEQUENCE

RECTILINEAR VISUAL FIELD

VISTA TOWARDS TOWN

GROUND LEVEL

From the ground level entry space, the visitor is drawn towards the ramp by its own overhang, then moving upward at the side of the core on the first orthogonal grid.

On moving along this first part of the ramp, the eye focuses on a panel of glass bricks. These are repeated at the opposite end to form an implied rectilinear visual field.

After the first landing, we are moving away from the core, with vistas into the town. Finally, after one last turn, we are moving along the new imposed grid and the ramp is stopped by the core. Its oblique alignment on plan links it visually with the core.

MOVEMENT SEQUENCE 2

AUDITORIUM

BALCONY

SECOND LEVEL

At the top of the ramp the visitor moves past the core towards either the curved viewing box, the triangular gallery, or more directly towards the auditorium.

Visitors start their introduction to New Harmony by seeing a film in the auditorium and on this direct route, movement is drawn by a view through a window directly ahead, then past a pivot door with a further view out; finally there is a right turn into the auditorium where a square window gives the last view out as visitors file to their seats.

This conclusion to the route, arrival in a contained box, is an appropriate termination of the movement sequence, psychologically representing arrival in a darkened enclosed space, in contrast to the openness of the route itself.

This final movement is directed by the curved stage edge, yet another counterpoint in the series of curves. Incised into this curve is a niche which marks out the orthogonal grid, the end of the stairs up to the stage and the start of the stairs to the gallery.

AUDITORIUM

AUDITORIUM

The auditorium is a sculpted rectilinear box in which the overhanging balcony becomes a device which keys in the stair ascending to it. The side gallery is incised into the adjacent side of the box.

The balcony edge extends in a very subtle gesture obliquely on the second grid along the longer side of the box at higher level. The major oblique in the box is the sloping floor with its regular rhythm of seats and the major shape in the box is that of the curved stage.

Only two colours are used to articulate these elements. A plain white is used for the walls, screen and main part of the ceiling, with a dark grey 'carpet' extending over the stage, seats and stairs.

THEME

230

The design theme for the Atheneum is concerned with the exploitation of the possibilities afforded by imposing a slight shift to an orthogonal grid. The dynamic thrust of the main imposed tilted plane sets up a tension within the cubic box which is strongly reinforced by having placed against it a series of horizontal triangular planes held by the oblique vertical plane which delineates a third geometry, that of the imposed square.

The main route is a particularly dynamic furtherence of the tilted grid, its linear force puncturing the planes of the orthogonal grid before meeting the main oblique plane.

Functional elements such as the curved viewing box, ramp, auditorium and entry box are deployed in accordance with their precise role and are treated accordingly. The curve of the viewing box responds to the river. The ramp is placed centrally to give access to the various levels. Deep back lighting is provided by the light well and by the rooflight cascade over the ramp. Further deep lighting occurs behind the oblique screen. Stairs reinforce both the main oblique thrust and superimposed implied square.

Individually and in their totality, forms, spaces, routes, views and light have a symbolic as well as a practical role. They demonstrate indirectly and abstractly those ideals with which Meier links the building with New Harmony's rich and complex past. He does not speak to us with obvious and banal references. Instead, he uses allegory and metaphor in the way the elements are organized and the way the building is sited so that we are made aware of the river on which the town was founded, the sense of order and harmony inherent in Rapp's vision, and the intellectual utopian commitment of Robert Owen.

JAMES STIRLING
EXTENSION TO
THE NATIONAL GALLERY, LONDON
competition entry

JAMES STIRLING

The work of James Stirling is characterized by its diversity and an eclecticism which can be traced back to his wide-ranging architectural interests as a student at the University of Liverpool.

As the architect explains, his interests 'oscillated backwards and forwards between the antique and the just arrived Modern Movement,'[1] and like Meier, Stirling acknowledges a debt to his teacher Colin Rowe. A fascination for English Baroque architects such as Archer, Vanburgh and Hawksmoor can be contrasted with an interest in the Constructivists and Le Corbusier. English Victorian architecture, Frank Lloyd Wright's concrete block houses and Johnson Wax building are other sources, as are English castles, French chateaux, Bavarian Rococo, Venetian palazzi and English country houses.

First in partnership with James Gowan, followed by a long association and partnership with Michael Wilford, Stirling quickly acquired an international reputation with a series of important buildings in the fifties and sixties. This has continued, with each decade reflecting current preoccupations. The Ham Common Housing pays homage to Le Corbusier's Maisons Jaoul; Leicester Engineering, Cambridge History and the Florey Building show an interest in a glazed skin and hard planar components; St Andrews University Residential Expansion is articulated in pre-cast concrete, whilst 'high tech' prefabrication is in evidence at the Olivetti Training School at Haslemere.

In the seventies and eighties, opportunities presented by competition-winning designs for buildings in strongly contextural situations in Europe and the United States have seen a change towards a greater attention given to massing and surface treatment. Again this reflects the general architectural shift away from abstract functional modernism towards a broader architectural canvas.

In these later works, as with the late work of Le Corbusier, Stirling has evolved an architectural language drawing on the breadth and depth of his interests. Again, as with Le Corbusier, the opportunities presented have coincided with already present skills in articulation together with a greater understanding of the role of architecture and particularly the effect of mass, space, surface, light and colour on the human psyche. The Staatsgalerie in Stuttgart, for example, makes reference to old and new, with 'Egyptian cornices, Romanesque windows, Constructivist canopies, ramps and flowing forms — a union of elements from past and present.'[2]

The unsuccessful competition submission by the Stirling Wilford partnership for the Extension to London's

---

[1] Taken from 'James Stirling: Architectural Aims and Influences', an address given at the ceremony for the presentation of the Royal Gold Medal by the Royal Institute of British Architects, R.I.B.A Journal, September 1980, pp. 36, 37.

[2] Ibid., p. 37.

National Gallery has been chosen to conclude
this study because it exemplifies the main
argument put forward in this book. This has
been to demonstrate that great architecture
depends on an understanding of architecture's
role in relation to both the past and the
present; on a sensitive response to programmatic
requirements in terms of the Genius Loci and
the prevailing culture; and also because the
project aptly demonstrates how 'layers' of
conceptualization can be revealed by diagrammatic
analysis (see James Stirling's Foreward to this book).

RICE UNIVERSITY 1979-81

SITE FORCES

As part of the triangle linked by the Mall, Whitehall and Birdcage Walk, and containing Buckingham Palace, Westminster Abbey and the Palace of Westminster, Trafalgar Square has considerable cultural significance. The presence of the National Gallery facing the Square adds an authority that becomes possible when a major art collection and the commemoration of a significant historical event combine in a key location.

Although flanked to east and west by substantial building masses, the square dissolves on its southern side, and the cultural forces are expressed through the media of the square and Gallery facade, which, despite the traffic flow and fragmented nature of the rest of the Square, act as a convincing symbolic ensemble. This is due to the way square and facade are locked together by symmetry and by the simple combination of monument, fountains and Wilkins' long facade, which acts as an urbane low-key backcloth, gaining in impact by its dominant position above the Square. Wilkins' use of the classical language with its distinctive hierarchy of elements, establishes the identity of the Gallery in a manner appropriate to the majority of its paintings, which were composed to a similar representational compositional code.

The key elements are the horizontal plane of the Gallery facade, punctuated by the central portico, set against the contained space of the square with its fountains, and the vertical feature provided by Nelson's column.

TRAFALGAR SQUARE

NATIONAL GALLERY

ST MARTIN-IN-THE-FIELDS

SOUTH AFRICA HOUSE

HAMPTON SITE

NELSON'S COLUMN

CANADA HOUSE

WHITEHALL

ADMIRALTY ARCH

THE MALL

NORTH

KEY ELEMENTS

237

NATIONAL GALLERY AND HAMPTON SITE

The principal facade of the National Gallery may be read as a plane with a rhythm of forward projecting pavilions. The three central pavilions express the main internal gallery circulation, whilst the central thrust of the entry portico defines the main lateral axis.

The dominant internal longitudinal axis, which also defines an important circulation route, is parallel to the external longitudinal axis which runs along the north side of the square. This internal axis provides a link opportunity to the proposed extension on the Hampton site, which is slightly wedge-shaped, diminishing at its southeastern corner, and there is a possible route through the site linking Trafalgar and Leicester Squares. (The route to Leicester Square ensures that Trafalgar Square forms part of the entertainment network of central London, giving a sense of one kind of node leading to another).

HAMPTON SITE

MAIN LATERAL AXIS

ST MARTIN-IN-THE-FIELDS

SECONDARY ZONE

DOMINANT INTERNAL LONGITUDINAL AXIS

EXTERNAL LONGITUDINAL AXIS

Although the extension site forms a potential stop to one end of the main Gallery facade, and can in this sense be compared to St. Martin-in-the-Fields, the two situations are quite different. Whereas the latter is in a relatively exposed position with its main longitudinal axis pointing towards the Gallery, the former is more enclosed and its main axis runs laterally at right angles to the longitudinal axis of the Gallery.

The site's location creates a link potential between it and Trafalgar Square, inducing a diagonal condition at the southeastern corner of the site. Because it is the access zone, visible from Trafalgar Square, this edge of the site offers the greatest potential for development. There is a secondary zone to the rear.

NATIONAL GALLERY

The Gallery may be read as a horizontal slab with a front and a back. This horizontality is furthered by the layering in which the plinth establishes a base, with a cornice defining the elevational 'canvas'.

An intermediate horizontal band separates the two rows of windows (the upper being blind) which animate the facade. Conforming to classical design principles, the elemental disposition is hierarchical, with clearly defined axes controlling the main gallery organization.

HORIZONTAL SLAB

HIERARCHICAL FACADE

MODULATED PLAN

Because of the length of the facade, the external profile of the plan is carefully modulated so that the main axes of the gallery arrangement receive external expression. This occurs in the pavilion-like projections identified by columns, and at entry by a pedimented portico with a dome immediately to the rear.

Care is given to stopping the facade at each end with first a projection surmounted by a dome, followed by a setback where the actual corner occurs. The twin domes at each end have a base which ensures a distinctly vertical thrust.

The surface treatment is low-key with a concern for balance between verticals and horizontals. Although the facade is predominantly horizontal the clusters of columns give localized vertical readings so that when viewed obliquely the facade emphasis becomes vertical.

The use of stone has several consequences for the National Gallery. The Gallery has a mass rather than a planar reading. In combination with the classical language, the use of stone gives the Gallery monumentality, authority and dignity. The sculpting of the mass with pilasters, cornice and columns gives considerable surface richness with the play of light and shadow.

THE EXTENSION

The generic form is linear in acknowledgement of the linear site axis, a static slab alongside the National Gallery. A pavilion projects forward, reduced in width because the site diminishes at this point.

The pavilion, aligned with the Gallery portico, picks up the forward-backward rhythm of the pavilion projections on the main Gallery facade. The form is now directional.

The remainder of the form is echeloned in support of the forward thrust, each setback being aligned with a gallery setback.

The front pavilion is aligned laterally and distinguished from the rest of the form by its upper treatment in which a pitched roof surmounts a section part-separated from the adjacent mass. This reinforces the lateral axis which runs parallel with the dominant internal axis of the Gallery and with the Gallery facade.

243

THEME

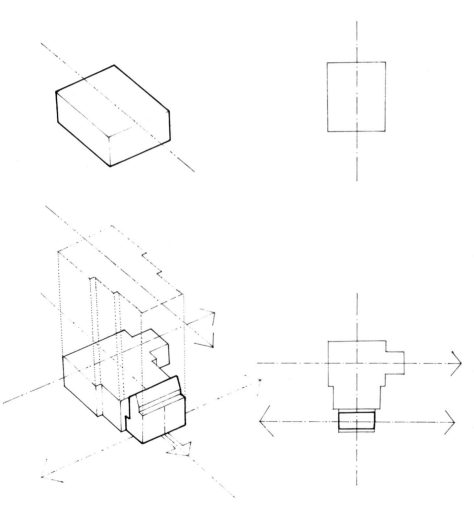

By separating the forwardmost projection of the echeloned mass, Stirling and Wilford recognize zonal differences in the site and establish a powerful contrast with the rest of the form which nevertheless remains part of the echelon system. This transforms a formerly static mass into a dynamic configuration, establishing the theme of the work, which is to exploit the opportunity afforded by a contextual situation to animate and dramatize one part of the form in contrast with the rest.

This dynamism is induced by the axial shift, and by the contrast of the vertical linearity of the forward pavilion when compared with the horizontal, slab-like remainder; opportunities for animation are provided by entry and by identification of the role of the building, particularly in relation to the existing Gallery.

The relationship between the pavilion and the rest of the extension affords a further opportunity to reconcile two geometric configurations, the symmetrical directional organization of the whole and the lateral thrust and part independence of the pavilion itself.

The theme is also concerned with the 'two worlds' encompassed by the programme, the Neo-classical world of the National Gallery and the twentieth-century world of the extension. This semantically rich opportunity is realized through the structure, materials and architectural language used in the extension.

PAVILIONS

The idea of the portico as a pavilion defining entrances is a major device employed by the Neo-classical buildings around Trafalgar Square.

Immediately opposite the site is the portico to Canada House whilst the portico of St. Martin-in-the-Fields provides a similar incident, this time acting as a stop to the east end of the Gallery facade.

The pavilion to Stirling and Wilford's extension stops the west end of the Gallery whilst being aligned so that the eastern end of the pavilion is placed on the centre of the portico opposite.

THE PAVILION

The lateral axis established by the alignment of the pavilion is reinforced by horizontal indentations in the facades, by a plinth and cornice which echo these features of the National Gallery, and by the pitched roof, which defines the axis. Although this linear emphasis echoes the main horizontal layering of the Gallery, it contrasts with the localized vertical reading at the south west corner, establishing a separate identity for the extension pavilion.

This separate identity creates a problem at the point of junction with the main configuration, particularly where the cornice meets the adjacent mass. This is resolved by attaching the cornice to the mass by two 'brackets', one at either end. This is reflected on the south side by indentations in the cornice so that when seen from above, it appears to have a flat top which joins the mass at either end and also at the centre.

The horizontal indentations in the Portland stone facade give it a 'mass' reading similar to that of a Renaissance palazzo (as the architects describe it). This is carried through with the provision of a base (plinth), middle and top (cornice) as with the National Gallery.

The forward pavilion may be read as a linear box, which becomes directional with the wedge-shaped opening in the lower part of the end facing the National Gallery. This erosion of the mass establishes a link with the space fronting the Gallery and (on oblique) with Trafalgar Square.

CANOPIES

If the wedge-shaped opening invites entry
and expresses a link with Trafalgar Square,
further definition of entry is added by twin
translucent projecting canopies.

These exert a linear rhythm, the more
forceful because two obliques are placed
alongside each other. Their shape, position,
length and translucent quality suggest that
they are sliding through the box rather
like those swords used by magicians who
'pierce' a lady in a box several times.

The canopy exerts further directional thrust,
reinforcing the linear axis and the link
with the space fronting the Gallery.

ALTERNATIVE DESIGN

In an alternative design submission (scheme C), Stirling and Wilford
proposed a forward pavilion with an angled projection which
picks up the alignment of Pall Mall East as it enters Trafalgar
Square. Compared with the preferred solution, this results in a
restless distortion of the forward mass, which, despite its echelon,
fails to lock satisfactorily into the rest of the configuration.

For this design the canopy is a simple pitched roof, giving a
serenity necessary to alleviate conflicts caused by the pavilion
which it fronts.

CIRCULAR STAGE

By opening up the box at one end, an inside/outside space is created. This opportunity is furthered by the circular place (described by the architects as a 'stage') which creates a kind of proscenium opening with a circular revolving stage.

This entire device, the wedge-shaped opening in the box and circular stage set into the podium, is a focus which pinpoints entry decisively, being supported by the translucent canopy above. The richness of the solution is compounded by the range of forms used and by their interacting energy components, which comprise: the dramatic and powerful opening into the box; the wedge-shaped 'embrace' of the sides; the stability/movement of the circular stage, itself given an added dimension by being half into and half out of the podium; and finally, in sharp contrast to the rest, the poised elevated thrust of the canopy, gaining in impact by being translucent, by having a double rhythm and containing twin obliques.

SOUTH FACADE

The south facade facing Pall Mall East has its mass reading broken through a double piercing by glazed bays which give views from the building along Pall Mall East and towards Trafalgar Square. It is as if the mass has been pulled sideways centrally. Delineating the dominant internal axis of the configuration, an oblique pointed form thrusts outwards, being surmounted by a more serene curved bay. This erosion also disrupts the cornice, now seen centrally as a slender plane, this being made explicit by the hole which reveals its depth.

The force of this disruption continues downwards, piercing the ground plane and podium in the form of an entry point at a lower level. This is reached by stairs, the outer boundary of which is set at an oblique angle, taking up the external direction of the pavement and of Pall Mall East.

As with the entry facade, elements are compressed together between plinth and cornice. The impact of these forms is increased by the fact that they are transparent (in contrast to the solidity of the mass which they pierce), and by the way their vertical rhythm of glazing bars contrasts with the horizontality of the facade indentations. In furtherence of this vertical/horizontal contrast a downward thrust is also in operation with the presence of a central column which pierces the floors behind the glass,

becoming external where it penetrates the baseline at plinth level. Although this column does not coincide vertically with the circular hole in the cornice, the one externalizes the other, the circular hole alluding to the idea of vertical penetration made manifest by the column.

The final directional thrust is at pavement level, where the oblique frame to the stairs giving entry to the shop completes the 'display' whereby a series of primary forms comprising transparent curved and oblique membranes in the vertical plane are juxtaposed against an oblique erosion of the ground plane in such a way as to animate and to an extent dramatize the ensemble.[1]

Four semi-circular windows are located in the plinth, giving light to the shop, this symmetrical deployment increasing the sense of monumentality, whilst the rhythm of curves gives a serene base, countering the dynamism of the punctured mass above. In this sense these windows belong first to the plinth or base, and also to the horizontal mode of the facade plane, their distinctive shape identifying their special function.

[1] This is similar to a familiar tactic in Le Corbusier's work whereby several contrasting forms are compressed together to dramatize a composition for a particular reason. See my analysis of the Monastery of La Tourette, Le Corbusier: An Analysis of Form. (Third Edition, 1996) E. and F. N. Spon, London.

DESIGN PRINCIPLES

The windows, in common with several other major elements in the design, perform several roles. These may be defined in terms of the way the theme of the work is interpreted by four constituents of the design strategy :

1. To ensure that every element observes the geometric properties of the configuration as a whole (this being an echeloned symmetrical mass with a directional thrust).

2. To ensure that every element in the design serves its particular function with a shape appropriate in usage and meaning.

3. To ensure that elements conform to what has been perceived as the overall function of the extension within its context and (more specifically) to the theme of the design. (To animate and dramatize one part of the form in contrast with the rest in terms of the 'two worlds' of the program).

4. To ensure that elements observe a correct relationship to their own particular part of the design, this to take account of the geometric characteristics and properties of each specific part of the design.

If we take these in turn in respect of the windows in the plinth :

1. The position of the windows supports the overall symmetry of the form

2. Their shape identifies a particular function, (that of lighting a space below ground level as opposed to giving a view out).

3. Their treatment (with keystones) has classical overtones which allude to the image of the building as a palazzo, this being part of the general perception of the relationship between the extension and the National Gallery.

4. Their semi-circular shape ensures a serene rhythm which supports the passive role of the plinth as the base and foundation of the composition.

MODERN AND POST-MODERN

Although the pierced cornice has Post Modern overtones in its ambiguous series of readings (solid from below, indentations from above), as does the explosion out of the box by twin transparent forms, the integrity of the Modern Movement functional credo is retained. This is evident in the way each device signifies a multi-faceted specific function (the upper fenestration gives a view out whilst recognizing internal differences of use – the curved bay signifies galleries whilst the oblique bay signifies the more animated movement at entry level). Similarly, the presence of a column which pierces each floor behind glass before emerging below the base plane of the pavement has both a Modern and Post-Modern flavour : Modern in the way a structural member behind glass shows the freedom given by twentieth century technology, Post-Modern in the device contradicts the mass reading of the 'palazzo.'

CONFRONTATION AND CORRESPONDENCE

The entire scenario of the extension thus sets out to confront its National Gallery neighbour with several propositions. First it is an independent adjunct, a point made by the architects who explain this in terms of its horizontality when compared to the nearest corner of the National Gallery: second it is linked to its neighbour not only physically, but also by its shape and alignment – the pavilion is symmetrical, it projects forward like the portico to the National Gallery and the mass reading and palazzo image correspond to these features of the National Gallery; third, in contradiction to these correspondences, the extension sets out to challenge its neighbour. Whereas the National Gallery is straightforward, uncomplicated, honorable and true, the south elevation of the extension is complex, has several layers of meaning, and is by comparison an intellectual puzzle which speaks through metaphor and allusion of present-day attitudes to history, art and technology.

PRIMARY FACADE

The design poses a problem as to which facade
(entry to the east or the Pall Mall facade) should
be primary. As expressed, the primary reading
is held by the entry facade by virtue of its
verticality and by the implied pediment provided
by the gable end to the pitched roof: as the
architects explain, the facade gains additional
force by being read as 'a face... looking
sideways towards the National Gallery, beyond
St. Martins-in-the-Fields, and obliquely into the
square.' [2]

This tactic relates to the architects' description
of the forward pavilion as 'the head on a body
where the rest of the anatomy does not have
the same density of external features.'[3]

The distinctive presence of a small clock face
confirms the symmetry of the gable and increases
the sense of 'personality' which, when combined
with the 'ears' of the cornice, makes this a
friendly and 'approachable' facade.

[2] Taken from the architects' comments in their explanatory
article, Architectural Design, 56 1/2 1986, p. 70.
This 'face' is similar to that used by Stirling and Wilford
in the Fogg Museum at Harvard University, see Architectural
Review, July 1986, pp 26-33.

3 Ibid p. 71

The generic slab has a ground-hugging boxiness that remains with the echelon transformation. Moves to diminish this are put in operation by breaking the rear mass at mid-point with a decisive erosion in the north-west corner to allow vehicle access under the form

DISTORTION

This device has several consequences. It confirms the 'back' reading of this part of the ensemble: raising the mass creates the impression that the rear boxes are no longer ground-hugging; it also significantly erodes a corner, which, although secondary to any reading towards Pall Mall or the square, can be read as opposite to these in importance or potential. The erosion also sets in motion an oblique, which, if carried through, continues towards Trafalgar Square.

The symmetrical echelon form is thus distorted by this turning motion. It is securely held by many other devices, particularly by the central thrust of the longitudinal axis, but there is pressure exerted on the form in a particular direction, i.e. towards the entry point where it faces Gallery and square, this being the main zone of the configuration.

MASS OR PLANES

WEST ELEVATION

This elevated section sets in being an implied continuity in the separation of upper from lower, expressed in the west elevation by fenestration incisions. These incisions affect the mass reading, particularly at the lower (entry) level where the mass dissolves into a series of planes.

This dichotomy, between a mass or planar reading for the rear of the configuration, is affected by the way the edge of the mass is raised above the flat roof to give a distinct skin or planar reading. This is furthered by the way the incisions push and pull in different directions suggesting both separation and linkage between the two boxes. This movement is stopped by the forward pavilion, although the incision immediately below the cornice bracket attaching it to the rear has its own forward thrust.

The result of these devices is that the elevation loses its mass reading and becomes taut and planar, although it is also part of a series of boxes, which by implication could all slide into each other.

SLIDING BOXES

The echelon form may be read as three boxes, each capable of sliding into the one behind. As if in acknowledgement of this possibility the centre box has its edge in the form of a zig-zag at entry level, this 'concertina' allowing the forward pavilion to slide back into the main slab.

This sliding is held by the rows of columns in the foyer which pin the box in position. The columns continue down to the baseline below

pavement level, their symmetry and shape signifying on the one hand circulation zones and on the other the structural principle of the building, which is to have a reinforced concrete frame and floor slabs with certain loads transmitted through columns.

The regular columnar rhythm of the foyer gives it a 'hypostyle hall' reading which combines order and formality with structural logic. Within a series of multivalent boxes the columns stabilize literally and metaphorically.

The movement progression from entry goes into a lobby towards a circular opening where the transverse and longitudinal axes meet. This sets in motion movement north along the axis into the transitional foyer zone leading towards the restaurant. From here movement dog-legs back again to the galleries above. The 'elasticity' of this zone signifies that it is a preparatory area at the centre of gravity of the configuration without a decisive directional or functional role. It mediates between back and front and, because of the stair location, between entry and gallery levels.

The stair is a major element, the main focal device of this spatial sequence, its central location and shape affirming the axis and its three dimensional and monumental presence identifying the movement route. By thrusting forward or back dependent on the main direction to be followed the stair becomes a vector of movement having considerable although muted energy. By its function it signifies not only its use but the predominant directional thrust of the building along the linear axis. The precise position of the stair enables it to move from box to box as appropriate, furthering the notion of interaction between the boxes. The movement axes create vistas which are appropriately terminated, the first by the cloaks, curved (in elevation); the second by the curve (in plan) of the restaurant wall. The finality of this restaurant wall signifies the end of movement and of the main circulation zone.

GALLERIES

PLAN AT GALLERY LEVEL NATIONAL GALLERY

THREE BOXES SEPARATED BY SIDE
WINDOWS DUCTS AND LIFTS CIRCULATION CORE

VISTAS IN GALLERIES CIRCULATION ROUTES

Above, the gallery level takes over the upper
section. This floor is bi-laterally symmetrical,
being controlled by the dominant linear axis.
This ensures a harmonious and serene disposition
of galleries with a series of vistas arranged
on the linear axis.

The form is self-contained with each of the three boxes 'separated' by side windows, ducts and lifts. This containment excludes the link, placed as a separate element on the transverse axis (dominant longitudinal axis of the National Gallery). The separate reading of the link is furthered by the curved exterior, which signifies that this is a special independent zone, neither Gallery nor extension.

The exterior curve in the form of a bay signifies a calm and restful zone. Throughout the design the various zones have a shape intended to signify their use, as for example the rest zone of the circle at entry, the inward movement identified by canopy and wedge shape, the holding areas in the lobby and foyer, followed by the calm, contemplative dignity of the galleries, whose vistas encourage movement in a slow and reflective manner.

The configuration has a circulation core around which the galleries are placed. The shape of the core contrasts with the outer echelon in having its major zone to the north, reversing the general directional thrust of the pavilion. This 'holding' zone is, however, at a centre of gravity between extension and National Gallery, its size warranted by its location and role. Columns define the major spaces and reinforce the general bi-lateral symmetry and identify circulation zones.

LOWER LEVELS

At shop level the three boxes are clearly defined with a wedge picking up the special quality of the central circulation zone, whilst at the lower level the fan shape of the auditorium gives a further interpretation of the echelon idea, the squeezing of the fan maintaining the forward thrust. At each level columns signify circulation zones.

266

As seen in section, the forward pavilion has a vertical force, which
is expressed externally by the ridge of the pitched roof and internally
by the piling up of spaces (boardroom and information stacked at
the top), with the circular opening in the entry lobby looking down
to the shop. The column behind the glazed projections embodies the
vertical emphasis within the pavilion.

LIGHTING

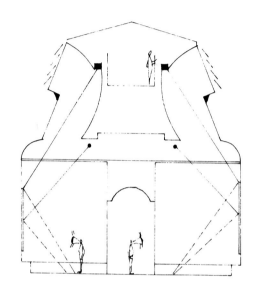

The lighting section for the galleries uses curves to give appropriate lighting and when combined with the use of curves inside the galleries, serves to give three-dimensional enrichment in a graceful manner, reinforcing the idea of dignity inherent in the gallery layout. The section also accommodates space for maintenance.

ROUTE AND BANNER

If the theme of the work is to exploit the configurational opportunities provided by the laterally thrusting forward pavilion within an overall linear echelon, the route under the link alongside the National Gallery ensures the primacy of the linear reading. Placed alongside the vigorous articulation of the masses this route is a calm, regular, absolutely straight movement vector whose slow pace does not diminish the significance of its role. Its serenity, cascading horizontality and strength of purpose gives it a vital position of contrast within the ensemble. In this, it echoes the dignity of the whole composition and particularly the gallery level of the extension, being similarly calm and yet assertive in a very low key manner.

The horizontal linearity and flat permanency of the route under the link alongside the National Gallery contrasts with the vertical fragility and transience of the banner at the southwest corner. But, as with the route, functional purpose is exploited to enhance the totality. The vitality of this triangular feature gives a visual link that is multi-directional and also by its 'scaffolding' and 'blowing in the wind' formation, contrasts effectively with the solidity of the extension. This addition is a far more satisfactory response to the wedge-shaped corner than the distortion of the forward mass as seen in Scheme C.

The banner strengthens a corner which is exposed by the wedge shape at this part of the site, it's triangular shape on plan extending the play of obliques in the design established by the roof pitch, the projecting glazed membrane at entry, the edge to the stairs down to the shop at pavement level and by the wedge shaped walls at entry.

DEVELOPED DESIGN

INITIAL   DESIGN

DEVELOPED   DESIGN

There are two main changes to the design as first submitted. First and most significant is the addition of the central drum to the pavilion. This is intended to give additional weight so that the extension may more happily balance with its opposite number, St. Martin-in-the-fields.

Second, the entrance configuration is no longer wedge-shaped with canopies. Instead, the circular 'stage' has been reinforced by curves which now extend into the walls at each side of entry, and the centre is marked by a single column.

This use of the circle, in the form of a cylinder in the centre of the pavilion and reinforcement of the circular 'stage', has several consequences which materially affect the design. The central cylinder reduces the linearity of the pavilion, giving it a pronounced centroidality which, when coupled with the stone cladding to drum and pitched roof, increases the sense of mass.

The way the drum pierces the obliques of the roof with its potential to revolve strongly reinforces the central piercing of the south facade by the glazed membranes.

Just as the mass is pulled out to accommodate this, so too does the mass now explode through the roof, so that, as on the facade, the internal is externalized - the drum lights the boardroom and signifies its importance, the membranes also express internal roles and the upper curved bay and drum 'communicate' with each other.

PAVILLION TO PALAZZO

Although the mass is pierced so vigorously, it is strong enough to resist, and its stability is not threatened in any way, so that, on the contrary, the central addition adds power as does the juxtaposition of drum and portico on the National Gallery.

Despite the absence of a dome, the drum to the extension establishes a resonance with the National Gallery, the contradiction of the absent dome furthering the series of allusions already operating in the pavilion.

The change in character from the earlier proposal is a dramatic exploitation of the focal point where lateral and longitudinal axes meet, increasing both the monumentality and sense of historical association. The plugging of this focus changes the image decisively from pavilion to palazzo — always the architects' intention, but now confirmed.

S E A T O N   D E L A V E L   N O R T H U M B E R L A N D

The total cladding of stone with the rich surface pattern of joints and heavy cornice has a sense of compact power reminiscent of Vanbrugh's Seaton Delavel, similarly a piled up sculpted mass with considerable theatrical content, being similarly animated and full of incident.

There is also a similarity with Mastro Jacopo's S Maria dei Miracoli at Brescia, in which the drum is placed behind the plane of the main facade, itself symmetrical and with a central forward thrust developed flamboyantly at cornice level with a series of semi-circular arches. The composition is held by the twin doorways at either side and by the strength of the central elements including the drum, the potency of this configuration being due to the close juxtaposition of drum and facade plane (each contrasting elements) with the stability of the drum permitting liberties on the facade.

S   M A R I A   D E I   M I R A C O L I   B R E S C I A

273

STAATSGALERIE, STUTTGART

S T A A T S G A L E R I E   S T U T T G A R T

This is not dissimilar to the way the central drum of the
Staatsgalerie at Stuttgart allows Stirling and Wilford to
manipulate the forms immediately in front of it. The
potential of a drum to 'turn' gives the form in all these
examples of its usage a double reading; it is both
static and dynamic, stable and yet mobile.

DRUMS AND VISTA

LONGITUDINAL   SECTION

DRUMS

The cylindrical penetration of the mass at roof level continues with the cylindrical drum of the hole looking down from entry level to the counter of the shop, this stopping the downward thrust.

VISTA

On gaining entry, the vista is stopped with greater moment by the treatment of the facing wall containing the cloaks. This becomes unambiguously bi-laterally symmetrical with the positioning of the twin rectilinear counter openings below the curve, and with circular openings above each.

SCULPTED FORMS AND SPACES

This weighty penetration of the mass by cylindrical voids is echoed and contrasted by the piercing of the floors by the forward central column behind the glazed membranes. This seizes the opportunity present in the submitted Scheme A, but extends the idea into several further dimensions.

At the top the column is now directly below the hole in the cornice, and is slender and cylindrical. It changes at entry level to become square in plan, but turned so that the four edges of the square are most apparent; this sits on a cylindrical base up to plinth level comprising a drum surrounded by seats and concludes at shop level with a sturdy stone-clad cylinder.

The turned square column slots into the diagonal floor pattern at entry level which, along with the circular drum, signifies a holding zone. The metamorphosis of the column, changing to respond to each activity zone – simple elegant cylinder / tranquil galleries – turned square and 'rotating' seats / active entry zone – sturdy, structurally 'functional' cylinder / below ground, holding everything up – is typical of the design philosophy in which the potential of each element is exploited as a demonstration of sculptural and evocative virtuosity.

A similar development occurs at the entry point where a column acts as a central focus for the circular 'stage'. This also changes from having a cylindrical base to having a turned square plan above, which in combination with the revolving/static 'stage' has both rotational and stable readings.

The isolation of the column and its multifaceted profile remains consistent with the way the extension seeks to mediate between the two worlds of the program. In all the nearby Neo-classical buildings, the column is eloquently expressive. The porticos by Smirke Wilkins and Gibbs each speak symbolically of entry by reference to Greek and Roman, using base, fluting and capitals to make their point. Within their rectilinear portico format they each enframe views outwards.

Similarly, within a circular format, Stirling and Wilford's column makes its own statement of entry and is consistent to its circular geometric frame, in its singularity perhaps referring to another column in Trafalgar Square.

The central location of a single column also delineates the axis of the palazzo in a way which necessitates not two but one cylindrical entry point, with a consequent funnelling of movement into a potential bottleneck.

Niches on the side walls amplify the curvilinear theme and inset windows reinforce the bi-lateral symmetry. The cylindrical base is up to plinth level, the turned square column locking into the diagonal floor plan of the initial holding zone.

WEST ELEVATION

The palazzo now forms part of a more homogeneous whole by virtue of a continuation of the incised courses along the rest of the configuration, although the rear boxes are not stone-clad. The pulling/pushing movement has gone as the design has become more static and monumental. The Modern Movement functional overtones recede as the ensemble concentrates instead on harmony and 'commodity'

Yet there are echoes of Modernism with the horizontal stretched windows in the rear box, which contrast with the insistent vertical rhythm of three pairs of inset windows. The symmetry of this group slows down the prevailing horizontality and increases the mass reading. Similarly four pairs of windows set up a symmetrical rhythm on the palazzo, this being supported by the three semi-circular basement windows. These devices encourage an independent reading of the palazzo. As in the first submission the elevation can be divided into a calm upper and an animated lower zone, the latter now containing a considerable variety of fenestration.

Something similar happens on the south elevation with the positioning of twin rectilinear windows on each side of the central gallery bay. These light the boardroom suite and also by their alignment point towards Trafalgar Square. As with any small opening in a mass they increase rather than diminish the mass statement.

The arcuated basement windows are more subdued than in the first submission and now without keystones, their curvilinear rhythm enriching the plinth, now raised to match that of the National Gallery. The external profile of the building increases the sense of plasticity and when combined with the surface treatment enriches the form.

DESIGN STRATEGY

In any important city centre location, the greatest architectural problem lies in the external image which a building presents. By comparison, the interior is easy; modern architecture has won many advantages over Neo-classical in the organization of circulation and space, the provision of effective lighting and the elimination of pretentiousness and monotony. But the outside remains a problem; the Modern Movement and its successors have not yet convincingly managed to emulate the architecture of previous periods in giving an appropriate cultural identity for major works in historic locations.

Stirling and Wilford have attacked this problem, chiselling out a plan profile for their extension which picks up the outline of the National Gallery, pushing a pavilion forward which fulfils a similar role to the portico of its neighbour whilst managing to project a friendly face towards Trafalgar Square as inviting in its message as its portico but without its overblown cultural implications. The pavilion also stops Wilkins' long facade at its west end in a similar manner to the way St Martin-in-the-Fields stops the east end.

A favorite device in London's Neo-classical buildings is the use of deeply recessed coursework in stone. This gives scale, increases the impression of mass and, as part of the classical language, has an inbuilt authority which gives that sense of importance so appropriate in a capital city. This is not copied but is alluded to in the Stirling Wilford extension in a way which sets up a similar mass reading but, by the wide separation of the courses, establishes an undisputed contemporary identity for the building.

This is typical of the design strategy in which, throughout, Stirling and Wilford play a subtle game of cross-reference between the extension and its neighbour, and thereby between past and present, reinforcing key items in the National Gallery such as the need to provide serene and dignified galleries, but enhancing the external modelling by its bag of twentieth-century tricks which include penetration of the box, exploitation of contrasts between mass and plane, geometrical transformations and distortions, a pediment in a kind of metamorphosis, not to mention a series of allusions and metaphors, some direct, some indirect, to its neighbour, to art and to creativity.

But all this is done within a framework of formality; plans and sections exhibit strict geometrical control, observing those correct <u>principles</u> of classical architecture which insist on the establishment of a carefully controlled movement sequence based on the vista and modulated by an observance of axes and by a studied disposition of elements.

In their more recent work the Stirling Wilford partnership in common with the Post-Modern movement has been exploring the possibilities of mass and surface with the intention of communicating with a wider audience. Their approach has reversed several Modern Movement canons as the late twentieth-century mood swings towards a more romantic range of expression.

Where the Moderns gave structure an almost moral role central to the logic of the program, this now changes so that columns, for example, express a multitude of meanings. Where symmetry was usually avoided it is now exploited. Often entrances were played down, now they can be celebrated. Where the Modernists used geometry as an overriding discipline, this is now sublimated to serve rather than control. From the harsh Constructivist geometry of Stirling's early works and the inherent hostility apparent in the search for consistency in a pure but limited design sense, the expressive range now extends towards form and surface seen psychologically as friendly or serene and having a capacity to endure.

Stirling and Wilford now part company from Post-Modern clichés in the seriousness with which they draw from source. Their statements are not platitudinous, but instead seek as did the Victorians, to use history in an appropriate way, mixing traditional forms such as the drum with late twentieth-century geometrical freedom.

Colin St. John Wilson has argued that architecture is born of use, and that it invents forms that celebrate a way of life', insisting that the message of the work must be recognizable in an intelligent way. The integrity of the Stirling Wilford proposal resides in the way the geometrical organization and modelling of the form respond to the precise needs of the building in both a functional and symbolic sense. The galleries are tranquil receptacles for works of art; the circulation has a subdued grandeur which is consistent with the syntax of the general arrangement in which forms and spaces convincingly explain themselves. The design, like that of the National Gallery, is rather low-key but with a dynamism and freshness of spirit which seek to provide a civilized and unpretentious ambience for the viewing experience.

6

SCIENCE, PHILOSOPHY, ART AND ARCHITECTURE

SCIENCE AND TECHNOLOGY

The twentieth century has been dominated by the relentless progress of science, and it is science that has provided mankind with ways of understanding and means of solving problems that have changed his perception of the world. Health, agriculture and food supply, communications and transportation, have all been transformed by the new technology, so that we now see the world through a scientific 'filter' as all-encompassing and pervasive as the power of religion in the middle ages.

Science has become the new God, leading Western man inexorably towards a modernity characterized by agnostic rationalism and a materialistic commercialism that voraciously consumes nature's resources. Within three centuries, Western man has distanced himself from the cycle of toil and contact with the land and the elements, so that he now exists in an increasingly artificial environment, largely independent of the former constraints imposed by nature.

Man's domination of nature, and opportunities created by science and technology that have been fuelled by capitalism, have improved the quality of life in a materialistic sense. The corollary of this has been an impoverishment of the spiritual dimension, with myth and ritual often reduced to a re-enactment of discredited beliefs.

The dilemma posed by the spiritual vacuum resulting from scientific progress has instigated an intense philosophical debate with considerable creative fall out. Two contrasting positions have emerged, the one being a nihilistic denial of traditional values and institutions, reappraising man's condition under the headings of poststructuralism and deconstruction. The other point of view seeks a return to our cosmic roots so that man may re-connect with a greater whole that science and technology have obscured, an approach furthered under the headings of hermeneutics and phenomenology.

'As a professional scientist I am fully committed to the scientific method of investigating the world. I believe science is an immensely powerful procedure for helping us to understand the complex universe in which we live. History has shown that its successes are legion, and scarcely a week goes by without some new progress being made. The attraction of the scientific method goes beyond its enormous power and scope, however. There is also its uncompromising honesty. Every new discovery, every theory is required to pass rigorous tests of approval by the scientific community before it is accepted... Generally science leads us in the direction of reliable knowledge.'

Paul Davis, The mind of God, Science and the search for ultimate meaning, Simon and Schuster, London, 1992. p. 14.

'In the eighteenth century modern technology, the practical incarnation of science, was born. First in England and then across Europe the Industrial Revolution took hold. The machine age began as man discovered his strength need no longer be that of his arm alone nor his speed that of his feet. Factories and railways filled out the net of knowledge which science had cast over the landscape. Richard Trevithick, Josiah Wedgwood and Benjamin Franklin were the solid, curious, energetic inheritors of the world that Descartes, Galileo and Newton had made. Blindness, alchemy, fragility and God were forgotten as the practical men took over. Scienza Nuova was translated into the new science and it worked...
Rural areas became depopulated as the peasantry abandoned the land to become the urban proletariat. The idea of the machine, a mute, efficient man-made realization of the eternal laws of science, became the dominant idea in the European mind. Machines promoted efficiency which created wealth in one vast impersonal mechanism... Technology was, above all, the ultimate, unarguable assertion of science's one big claim: it works.

Bryan Appleyard, Understanding the present: science and the soul of modern man. Picador, London, 1992. p. 69

SCIENCE AFFIRMED

The aesthetic implications of the scientific revolution were articulated with visionary passion by the Futurists. In May, 1914, the young Italian architect Antonio Sant'Elia exhibited designs for a New City. He accompanied this with a Messagio that advocated an architecture true to the changed world of the twentieth century. These ideas became central to the Futurist's credo and were remarkably prophetic as an outline philosophy and in detail, projecting an image of an architecture that would be realized six decades later in the style known as High Tech.

The following are extracts from Sant'Elia's Messagio:

> The problem of Modern architecture is not a problem of rearranging its lines; not a question of finding new mouldings, new architraves for doors and windows ... But to raise the new-built structure on a sane plan, gleaning every benefit of science and technology, settling nobly every demand of our habits and our spirits, rejecting all that is heavy, grotesque and unsympathetic to us (tradition, style, aesthetics, proportion), establishing new forms, new lines, new reasons for existence, solely out of the conditions for Modern living, and its projection as aesthetic value in our sensibilities...
>
> Such an architecture cannot be subject to any law of historical continuity. It must be as new as our state of mind is new, and the contingencies of our moment in history...
>
> We must invent and rebuild ex novo our Modern city like an immense and tumultuous shipyard, active, mobile and everywhere dynamic, and the modern building like a gigantic machine. Lifts must no longer hide away like solitary worms in the stairwells, but the stairs — now useless — must be abolished, and the lifts must swarm up the facades like serpents of glass and iron. The house of cement, iron and glass, without carved or painted ornament, rich only in the inherent beauty of its lines and modelling, extraordinarily brutish in its mechanical simplicity, as big as need dictates, and not merely as zoning rules permit, will no longer lie like a doormat at the level of the thresholds, but plunge storeys deep into the earth, gathering up the traffic of the metropolis connected for necessary transfers to metal cat-walks and high-speed conveyor belts.
>
> Quoted from: Reyner Banham, Theory and Design in the First Machine Age, Architectural Press, London, 1960, pp. 128, 129.

Sant'Elia's vision captures the dynamism and power of science in a direct assimilation of its most evident benefits. Power stations, hydraulic dams and interconnected transport systems are the inspiration for an aesthetic whose forms, rhythms, pattern and scale emanate from steel trusses, concrete structures and modular glazing.

Past styles are eliminated at a stroke as the elegant structures offer enhanced possibilities for living, work, leisure and transport.

Antonio Sant'Elia, La Città Nuova, 1914. (after Sant'Elia).

THE ARTIST AND THE SCIENTIST

I think it is fair to say, that of all the architects practising in the last decades of the twentieth century, no one has done more, by pronouncements and buildings, to realize the Futurist vision of an architecture inspired by science and technology, than the English architect, Sir Richard Rogers.

In 1989, at a symposium held in New York, Richard Rogers explained his point of view in a talk entitled 'The artist and the scientist.'[1] The following are extracts from his paper:

> The twentieth century is a period dominated by innovation and the spirit of science. It has had revolutionizing effects on all fields of man's endeavour — art, economics, and politics. Through the unprecedented scale of scientific change, the world is becoming an artifact, an industrial village. Once dominated by nature, the world's surface is now covered by an immensely complex network of micro information and traffic links. Our inability to comprehend the implication of this change to a technically unified world lies at the very heart of world crisis.
>
> A fundamental problem of contemporary architecture is that it hasn't moved forward fast enough to keep up with science and technology. To overcome this, our office calls together all the relevant specialists, including the consultant engineers, the moment we get a project. These engineers help to analyse the problem at a strategic level, in such a way that it gives us a handle on the architecture. Thus contemporary science provides a tremendous base for the aesthetics we use. Today architecture is a matter not of an artist working in a garret but of teamwork and synthesis.

In the paper, Rogers justifies his approach by describing how his partnership designed the Extension to London's National Gallery in Trafalgar Square (first competition in 1982). The design team concluded that the National Gallery was a 'mediocre classical building' surrounded by other mediocre types, the only good building fronting onto the square and the National Gallery being St. Martin-in-the-Fields' with its great spire by John Gibbs.' Accordingly Rogers proposed a modern tower to relate to St. Martin's spire, this giving a view across London and at its base, emphasizing the entrance to the new gallery, this being raised to provide a 'triumphal arch as an entrance to Trafalgar Square.' In the spirit of Sant'Elia's comprehensive approach to the Città Nuova, Rogers proposed a major route linking Leicester and Trafalgar squares, with a new galleria below the existing road opening out in Trafalgar Square.

[1] Richard Rogers. 'The artist and the scientist,' Bridging the Gap, Building Arts Forum, New York, Proceedings edited by Deborah Gans, Van Nostrand Reinhold, New York, 1991, pp. 139, 140.

Richard Rogers Partnership. Competition entry for the extension to the National Gallery, Trafalgar Square London, 1982.

VENTURI AND SCOTT BROWN

Richard Rogers' scientific 'reading' of the world, leading him to an architecture that resembles machines, may be compared with the architectural language of early modern architects such as Le Corbusier, who, during the twenties, also celebrated the machine in an architecture of abstraction (derived in Le Corbusier's work from the artistic and philosophical movement known as Purism).

This approach, with its honest expression of the parts of a building (stairs, ramps, 'ribbon' windows and roof terraces became the icons of modernism — in Rogers' work stairs, escalators, lifts, ducts and structure fulfil a similar role) had been analyzed by Robert Venturi, whose book Complexity and Contradiction in Architecture (see pages 54, 55) argued for an architecture that drew on historical precedent to produce 'a complex and contradictory architecture based on the richness and ambiguity of the modern experience.'

Venturi's preference for the 'compromising rather than the clean' and for 'hybrid rather than pure' attacked the puritanical morality and consequent sterility of orthodox modern architecture. The critique singles out the 'less is more' approach of Mies van de Rohe, but acknowledges the richness of multiple readings and ambiguities in works by Le Corbusier and Alvar Aalto.

Robert Venturi and Denise Scott Brown won the second stage of the competition to extend the National Gallery with a design that aptly demonstrates Venturi's argument. The Venturi's Sainsbury Wing of the National Gallery exemplifies the gulf between their world-view and that of Richard Rogers, pointing up differences in their respective perceptions regarding cultural specificity (the uniqueness of cultures as opposed to any global reading), the relevance of history and the importance of context. At all events, a key distinction between the Rogers' and Venturi's solutions is that the former is assertive, making no concessions to the National Gallery, whilst the latter defers and clearly respects the seniority of the primary gallery.

The Venturi's Sainsbury Wing of the National Gallery seems at first to be reactionary and anachronistic, a neo-classical building displaced from its time. In fact, it belongs to the present and the past, having all the complexity, contradictions and ambiguities outlined by Robert Venturi in his seminal work three decades earlier.

The National Gallery and the wedge shaped site for the extension were the points of departure for the concept. An oblique axis is formed, offset from the orthogonal geometry of the National Gallery and a cranked entry zone faces Trafalgar Square. This zone has a radial double skin, the outer being masonry, with large voids for entry and the inner being glazed with views of the foyer and restaurant on different levels. This is reversed internally at the main stair (alongside the National Gallery), which has an outer glazed skin and an inner masonry wall—reflecting the wall of the National Gallery opposite. This layering of the external skin reminds us of Venturi's reference in <u>Complexity and Contradiction</u> to the complex layering in Baroque architecture. [1]

There are references to both historical and modern architecture as the building responds to subtle nuances of the site and to idiosyncratic aspects of the English culture. Although entirely of its time, the Sainsbury Wing resonates with memories of the rich heritage of Western civilization, and the Italianate mood of the building establishes a relationship with the early Renaissance collection housed in its galleries. Thus the Sainsbury Wing validates the idea of historic continuity, providing a sympathetic ambience to a unique collection of paintings whilst giving fresh life to a 'much loved friend' (to quote Prince Charles).

Robert Venturi and Denise Scott Brown, The Sainsbury Wing of the National Gallery, London, 1991.

[1] See my analysis of the Sainsbury Wing in <u>Architectural Design Profile No. 94</u> edited by Andreas C Papadakis, St Martins Press, New York, 1991 pp 16-19

CONSTRUCTIVISM

Throughout the twentieth century, themes of modernism have evolved, inspired by the machine (and the technology of production), by modern art and by perceptions of social progress. In the years immediately following the Russian Revolution, the aspiration towards an egalitarian society was seen in terms of the transformation of a peasant economy into a modern industrial state.

Unlike the Italian Futurists, whose visions were graphic rather than structural, the Russian Constructivist movement brought together evolving concepts in abstract art with the constructive demands initiated by the new technology. This focus on the pragmatic and the aesthetic, intending to realize a powerful social ideal, became one of the most inventive architectural movements of the century, its imaginative potential being realized in the 'eighties and 'nineties by deconstructivist architects such as Bernard Tschumi and Coop Himmelblau, and in the dynamic concepts of Zaha Hadid.

It was Vladimir Tatlin who first crystallized the spirit of the Revolution, with his monument to the Third International (1919-20). The monument consisted of an ascending spiral wrapped around two connecting axes. Within this iron framework, glazed volumes revolve in perpetual motion, each operating at different speeds.

Thus the former solidity and immutably static nature of monumental civic architecture was eliminated, being replaced by a prismatic skeletal statement of iron and glass that represented movement and time. Although unrealized in other than model form, this is undoubtedly one of the most provocative and revolutionary architectural images of the twentieth century, symbolizing liberation by art, by engineering, by new materials and techniques, and by socialism. It is this connection between art and everyday life that is most significant in Constructivism, bringing those usually separate fields of art and industry together, to reflect its period in an unusually powerful manner.

DEFINITION OF CONSTRUCTIVISM

Constructivism is the organisation of the given material on the principles of tectonics, structure and construction, the form being defined in the process of creation by the utilitarian aim of the object.

From the Constructivist magazine LEF 1923

MONUMENT TO THE THIRD INTERNATIONAL
A contemporary description :

The whole monument rests on two main axes which are closely connected. In the direction of these axes an upward movement is accomplished; this is crossed transversely at each of its points by the movement of spirals... The chambers are arranged vertically above one another and surrounded by various harmonious structures. (The glazed mobile elements). By means of special machinery they are to be kept in perpetual motion but at different speeds. The lower chamber is cubiform and turns on its axis once a year; it is to be used for legislative purposes... The chamber above is pyramidal in shape and makes one revolution a month; this is for the meetings of assemblies and executive bodies. Finally the third and highest part of the building is in the shape of a cylinder and turns on its axis once a day. This part of the building will be used chiefly for administration and propaganda, that is, as a bureau, for newspapers, manifestos,

Vladimir Tatlin model of monument to the Third International 1919-20.

etc. Telegraphs and radio-apparatus and projectors for cinematographic performances will be installed in this chamber...

Kenneth Frampton 'Notes on a Lost Avant-Garde' Arts Council catalogue to Art in Revolution, Soviet Art and Design since 1917, Hayward Gallery, London, 1971, pp. 21, 22.

THE CONSTRUCTIVISTS

Vesnin brothers. Project for Pravda building 1923-24.

'Such was the crazy, intoxicated atmosphere of this <u>avant-garde</u> world in Pre-Revolutionary, war-time Russia. Exhilarated by a sense of power, tremendous optimism, and a giddy excitement as they stood on the brink of a new world, they yet found themselves unable to communicate this excitement to the society in which they found themselves.'[1]

The Leningrad Pravda newspaper building, designed by Alexander Vesnin and his brother Victor, has been described by Kenneth Frampton as comparable 'as a canonical work with... Le Corbusier's Ozenfant studio, Rietveld's Schroeder house or Mies van de Rohe's glass skyscraper project, all of the years 1922-23.'[2] In all these examples, the new technology defined an aesthetic drawn from art: In Le Corbusier's case, from Purism, for Rietveld, Di Stijl, and for Mies van de Rohe, Suprematism.

The Pravda building, with its digital clock, searchlight, rotating billboard and external elevators, despite its synthesis of the tectonic and the industrial, derived its celebration of the mechanistic, and especially movement, from artistic developments that pre-dated the Revolution.

The Cubism of Picasso and Braque had been the point of departure for Suprematism, introduced by Kasimir Malevich at an exhibition in Petrograd in 1915. (at which Tatlin also exhibited). Malevich and other Russian artists, transformed the shifting planes and multiple viewpoints of Cubism into dynamic thrusting planes whose impetus was primarily that of movement.

[1] Camilla Gray, <u>The Russian Experiment in Art, 1863-1922</u>, Thames and Hudson, London, 1962 p. 215

[2] Kenneth Frampton, 'Notes on a Lost Avant-Garde', <u>Art in Revolution</u> Arts Council Exhibition catalogue London 1971 p. 24

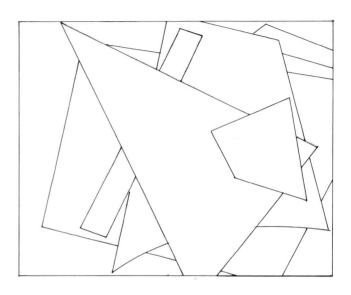

ART AS LIBERATION

Kasimir Malevich, <u>Dynamic Suprematism</u>, 1916
(in greys, yellow, blue, black, white, cream, brown, rust and orange)

Luibov Popova, <u>Architectonic Painting</u>, 1917. (diagram of composition).
(in vermilion, purple, brown, rust, black and cream)

In Malevich's <u>Dynamic Suprematism</u>, shapes seem to hover around a triangular 'module' as if they are floating in space. Unlike Cubist painting, with its ambiguities and compaction within a frame, in Suprematist works the planes are perceptually clear and without constraints, resisting the restriction of a frame. Malevich saw the machine as liberating man from the tyranny of nature and distanced himself from conventional attitudes towards meaning, resulting in an absolute level of detachment and abstraction.

Malevich described the space within his paintings as without human measure. As stars within the cosmos, these colour-bolts move upon an appointed way, irrevocable, inevitable. It is not a moment of nature held on canvas, nor an ideal world existing independently, it is a corner of the cosmos caught on its journey through time.[1]
Luibov Popova is regarded as the outstanding painter of the post 1914 abstract schools in Russia. Camilla Gray has described her Architectonic Paintings of 1917-18 : They leave 'the impression of a lightning-swift movement, a darting, breathless meeting of forces, a kiss-imprint, as it were, of the driving energy around us.'[2]

[1] Camilla Gray, The Russian Experiment in Art, 1863-1922, Thames and Hudson, London, 1962, p. 166   [2] Ibid., p. 204.

295

THE RATIONALISTS

Alongside (and sometimes confused with) the Russian Constructivist movement, was the Rationalist movement. Like the Constructivists, the Rationalists were inspired by experiments in painting by Malevich, El Lissitsky and others. Nikolai A. Ladovsky advanced the theory of a rational architecture, in which clearly discernable forms were articulated in ways that would be readily perceived by an observer, such forms having no reference to past associations.

The Rationalists believed that architectural space could be redefined in terms of the interaction of planes, and they drew on Malevich's spatial concepts in his paintings, and on the lucidity of his forms.

Rationalist design principles were formulated in the studios of the Moscow Vkhutemas (Higher Technical Studios) and a design by I. I. Volodko introduced the idea of interpenetrating planes arranged on the diagonal. This design embodies the perceptual clarity, spatial flow, planar interaction and dynamism with the use of diagonals that comprised the Rationalist credo. It was also a completely abstract concept.

These principles informed the work of Konstantin Melnikov, being realized in his Soviet Pavilion for the Exposition of Decorative Arts and Industries in Paris (1925). This building, like the Pravda newspaper project, proved influential in the evolution of modern architecture. Like Le Corbusier's Pavillon de l'Esprit Nouveau (at the same exhibition), the Russian pavilion stood out as an example of the use of contemporary materials, geometry, abstraction and space amidst the eclectic stylistic pavilions of other countries.

I. I. Volodko Second year exercise, a covered market, 1923 (at the Vkhutemas school in Moscow).

Konstantin Melnikov Russian pavilion at the Paris International Exhibition 1925

VLADIMIR KRINSKY

Vladimir Krinsky, Project for a Tribune, 1921

Coop Himmelblau, Penthouse Pavilion at the Groningen Museum in the Netherlands, 1994.

The Penthouse Pavilion, using a Deconstructivist approach, echoes the spirit and the aesthetic of Krinsky's Tribune in its flouting of the conventional and by its fragmented, distorted image. Wolf Prix, of Coop Himmelblau, has described how shipbuilding techniques were used to build the museum, using steel panels that in a hundred years would have rusted away, leaving the art outside the building. He describes how bridges intentionally destroy the view and how a mistake in the original drawings is preserved in the form of a useless enclosed courtyard.[1]

[1] Wolf Prix was speaking at the Bartlett school in London, reported by Kester Rattenbury in Building Design November 8th 1994, p 17.

The ideas of the Rationalists were also advanced by Vladimir Krinsky, a co-founder of the movement, his Tribune project drawing on Cubism in the complexity of its planar composition.

The Tribune abandons traditional concepts of structure and form, and as with Malevich's Suprematist paintings, the project conveys a liberated form of dynamism in departing from conventional principles of order and by its total abstraction.

This unorthodox destruction of accepted canons was furthered in Krinsky's skyscraper design, which again abandoned structural and compositional conventions as the building is twisted and broken into disparate parts.

Vladimir Krinsky Project for a skyscraper for the V S N K H 1923.

ZAHA HADID

Zaha Hadid Residence for the Irish Prime Minister Dublin 1980.

¹quoted from Zaha Hadid, Planetary Architecture 2, Architectural Association, London, 1983.

Perhaps the most striking expression of optimism and confidence in the twentieth century is evident in the work of Zaha Hadid. Inspired by the Suprematist images of Malevich and Popova, and especially by the work of Leonidov, Hadid's projects possess a dynamism and energy that she sees as representative of the spirit of the age.

Camilla Gray's description of Popova's 'lightening swift movement' and 'darting breathless meeting of forces, a kiss-imprint... of the driving energy around us' is realized architecturally throughout Hadid's work, occasionally seeming to be literally derived from Russian sources.

If we compare Popova's Architectonic Painting (1917) with Hadid's Residence for the Irish Prime Minister in Dublin (1980), the thrusting triangle and 'floating' planes of Popova are captured in Hadid's design. She describes her approach:

'I wanted to push the notion of explosion in architecture and that's what this project really taught me - pushing a thing to a certain limit where it doesn't become ridiculous, where you are very much in control, and it erupts only where it is possible. I began to develop my own language, something which was quite personal... You have an existing walled garden... The triangle has a certain force and if that then hits a wall, certain things erupt, due to a sheer physical power... it's only in these moments that things begin to burst. I had... to break certain barriers.'¹

'It was in 1976, towards the end of my fourth year at the Architectural Association that I came to realize that architecture's role had yet to be fulfilled and that there were new territories which were yet to be explored.

The twentieth-century triumph of technology and our accelerating and ever-changing life styles have created a totally new condition. These changes, despite the difficulties, have a certain exhilaration which is yet to be matched in architecture. It is that revision and the absolute need for inventiveness, imagination and interpretation that makes our role in architecture more valid. We can no longer fulfil our obligations as architects if we carry on as cake decorators. Our role is far greater than that. We, the authors of architecture, have to take on the task of reinvestigating modernity.

An atmosphere of total hostility, where looking forward has been, and still is, seen as almost criminal, makes one more adamant that there is only one way and that is to go forward along the path paved by the experiments of the early Modernists. Their efforts have been aborted and their projects untested. Our task is not to resurrect them but to develop them further... In every project there are new territories to be invaded and others to be conquered; and this is only the beginning!' [2]

2 Ibid., introduction to <u>Planetary Architecture 2</u>, Zaha Hadid, 1983

Zaha Hadid Hotel and retail complex in a competition for the development of a site at 42nd St. on Times Square New York 1995 (compare with Krinsky skyscraper 1923).

DECONSTRUCTION

There are close parallels between the Rationalist abandonment of accepted canons and the resultant aesthetic (as in Krinsky's projects) and the late 'twentieth century architectural style of Deconstruction.

THE STRUCTURALISTS

Architectural Deconstruction originated, by association, with the French literary and philosophical movement with the same name. The philosophy of Deconstruction emerged as a reaction against the movement known as Structuralism, first put forward by Ferdinand de Saussure in a series of lectures given at the University of Geneva between 1906 and 1911.

Saussure argued that language (words and sentences) provides us with a coherent way to organise our thoughts. Language allows us to establish systems of meaning and communication leading to a series of signs that enable us to understand the world. Saussure's successors included Claude Lévi-Strauss and Roland Barthes, who used his approach as a basis for a Structuralism that could relate to anthropology and to relations between kith and kin, incidents in myth and other phenomena.

THE POST-STRUCTURALISTS

Jacques Derrida, the founding father of Deconstruction, argued against the Structuralists by asserting that there is no consistent relationship between words and their meaning. Derrida set out to show that texts contain inherent conflicts that prevent them having any fixed meaning. He reveals this by 'deconstructing' them in order to reveal inconsistencies, a technique he applies to other academic disciplines.

JACQUES DERRIDA

In 1986, Derrida explained Deconstruction as:

> 'Something has been constructed; a philosophical system, a tradition, a culture, and along comes a de-constructor (who) destroys it stone by stone, analyses the structure and dissolves it ... One looks at a system ... and examines how it was built, which keystone, which angle... supports the building; one shifts them and thereby frees oneself from the authority of the system' [1]

Derrida asserts that much of what we build is involved in the re-enforcement and imposition of power structures already in place. He contends that there are no factual realities that transcend time - only interpretations; therefore we continue to return to a comfortable, supposed historic origin which refuses to examine the present as it is. He believes that the only way to correct this is to 'deconstruct' or to deliberately vandalize traditional values in order to liberate ourselves from ethnocentrism, logocentrism and phonocentrism.

According to Derrida, the built environment is based on a web of culture and language that has no foundation in reality - it is always based on false premises. He believed it was therefore necessary to re-examine traditional values by casting doubt on accepted conventions. This departure from accepted norms is seen as a necessary liberation, as the norms are, in any case, a sham. For Derrida, the ordinary world of Western traditions can be unmasked as not being real, the posturing of pure fiction as supposed reality. When extended to architecture, conventional precepts such as order, respect for an existing condition, compositional harmony or structural logic are abandoned in favour of the 'explosive' and open-ended approach of a Zaha Hadid or the subversive tactics of Coop Himmelblau or Peter Eisenman.

[1] quoted from Geoffrey Broadbent, Deconstruction: A Student Guide. Ed. Jorge Glusberg Academy Editions, London, 1991.

THE AVANT-GARDE

Derrida's questioning of conventional attitudes echoes the intentions of avant-garde architects who have sought to advance the exploration of the frontiers of architecture. Throughout the twentieth century the avant-garde have challenged the status quo, providing a stimulus that, in the visual arts, has greatly extended the range of aesthetic possibilities.

Picasso, Marcel Duchamp and Le Corbusier, to give but three examples, each saw the role of the artist as being to challenge the 'hypocrisy' of adhering to outdated attitudes in the modern age. If modernity has provided the stimulus, as Robert Hughes has pointed out, 'The wish for absolute freedom is one of the constants of intellectual life,' [1] and the much prized freedom of the artist has played a key role in the progress that has transformed the twentieth century. We can see this everywhere - in clothes, music, advertising, in the packaging of products, in attitudes and certainly in architecture. It is hard to separate the spirit of the work of Californian architect Eric Owen Moss, from the creative output of sculptors such as Anthony Caro, and this connection, between artist and architect, with its expansion of the creative imagination, is of inestimable value in our lives.

During recent decades, architectural education has proved to be one of the most fruitful 'laboratories' for experimentation, acting as fertile ground for the furtherance of avant-garde philosophy. Some schools have encouraged a spirit of enquiry, aptly summarized by Allen Cunningham in a discussion of the President's Medals awarded by the Royal Institute of British Architects for outstanding student projects: 'It is the general expectation that schools of architecture educate successive generations to think like architects and serve the profession productively. Okay, but the schools do much more by encouraging experimentation and subversion (necessary ingredients in all creative activities), as their contribution to the evolution of architecture.' [2]

[1] Robert Hughes, The Shock of the New, New York, 1981, p 212. [2] Allen Cunningham, Building Design, December 15, 1995, p 10

THE PRESIDENT'S SILVER MEDAL FOR THE BEST MAJOR DESIGN PROJECT

1995

Timothy Sloane, Bartlett School of Architecture, University College, London.
'Between Two Walls' Temporary buildings for tight infill sites in Hong Kong.

SYMBOLIC MISREADINGS

The avant-garde alignment with art and technology creates its own potent symbolism, with imagery acceptable to the cognoscenti but not necessarily understood by the layman. Le Corbusier's concept of the dwelling was initially inspired by his painterly explorations with Purism and by his belief that the dwelling should echo the spirit of machine technology.

We may contrast the failure of Le Corbusier's abstract language, as expressed in the Villa Savoye (page 54) or Villa Stein-de-Monzie (pages 68 and 69) with the success of Frank Lloyd Wright's Prairie Style homes. Wright's ground-hugging houses, with protective overhanging roofs, concentrated on the idea of shelter combined with the liberation of space. Wright used brick, stone, timber and reinforced concrete. He did not eliminate pattern and managed to convey an acceptable symbolism that satisfied deep seated psychological yearnings alongside desires for freedom and independence.

Although Wright was committed to the idea of progress and to the highest artistic standards, his sensitivity towards his culture and to specific regional, climatic and human concerns, separate him fundamentally from the far narrower ideology of the avant-garde.

The unacceptable abstraction of early modernism was followed, in the 'fifties by the New Brutalism, an extreme avant-garde movement inspired in part by artistic perceptions and by an intellectual preoccupation with the integrity of materials. The resultant use of steel, tough concrete, exposed ducting and plumbing was again rejected by a public that had never been consulted or properly considered in its inception. The problem is highlighted by symbolic misreadings, as when Sir Denys Lasdun's National Theatre in tough reinforced concrete is thought of by Prince Charles as resembling an atomic power station, and when Sir Richard Rogers' Lloyds Building, with external ducting is compared to an oil refinery.

An essential difference between art and architecture lies in the realm of responsibility. Art is completely liberated. It can be subversive, irresponsible and obscure. Sir Hugh Casson, an architect and former President of the Royal Academy of Arts, has referred to the 'ruthless obscurity' of much modern art. He likened much modern art to 'a party to which we have not been invited' saying that all too often artists are 'narcissistic and vain.'

Robert Hughes contrasts the failed Utopian city visions of architects with works by modern painters. Using Mondrian's Broadway Boogie-Woogie as his example (1942-43), he points out that the painting is a diagram of a kind of energy and order that can be seen 'beneath the quotidian chaos of the great flawed Metropolis.'[1] There is a grid, and Hughes explains how the yellow blips shuttling along their paths do not 'represent' cabs, but 'once one has seen Broadway Boogie-Woogie the view from a skyscraper down into the streets of New York is changed forever.'

Hughes continues:'and why should Mondrian's last paintings still move us whereas the Utopian city plans of architects do not?' Hughes explains that 'the space of art is the ideal one of fiction. In it, things are not used and they never decay ; one cannot walk in a painting as one walks through a street or through a building. The paintings are incorruptable. They are the real rudiments of Paradise, the building blocks of a system that has no relationship with our bodies, except through the ocular perception of colour.

Piet Mondrian Broadway Boogie-Woogie 1942-43

Architecture and design, on the other hand, have everything to do with the body—and the unredeemed body, at that. Without complete respect for the body as it is, and for social memory as it stands, there is no such thing as a workable or humane architecture.'

[1] Robert Hughes, The Shock of the New, New York, 1981, p. 204.

A PHENOMENOLOGY OF THE SOUL

We may contrast avant-garde preoccupations with science and technology, Deconstruction and art, with another, quite different point of view. Philosophers such as Martin Heidegger and Gaston Bachelard, dissatisfied with what they saw as the limited perceptions of scientific rationality, and in particular the failure of science to address intangibles relating to human feelings, turned to poetry as a means of investigating the world of our emotions.

Bachelard and Heidegger saw poetry as offering a more profound understanding of Susanne Langer's 'life of feelings' (p. 39) than scientific reasoning was able to do, and their philosophical outlook was informed by German poets such as Hölderlin, Rilke and George Trakl.

The French philosopher Gaston Bachelard distinguished between thought, with its implications of a logical understanding of phenomena based on knowledge and experience, and the poetic image, which, he points out 'comes <u>before</u> thought.'[1] Bachelard explains that he is seeking to define a 'phenomenology of the soul,' and he suggests that 'in many circumstances we are obliged to acknowledge that poetry is a commitment of the soul.'[2] He continues: 'Forces are manifested in poems that do not pass through the circuits of knowledge.'[3]

Bachelard set himself the task of investigating what we mean by such intangible concepts as 'home', and to fully comprehend 'the spaces we love.'[4] He addresses those images of intimacy' that 'pose the problem of the poetics of the house.'[5] Far from seeing the house in Le Corbusier's scientific terms as 'a machine for living in,' he sees it instead as 'a tool for the analysis of the human soul.'[6]

[1] Gaston Bachelard, <u>the Poetics of Space</u>, Beacon Press, Boston, 1969, p. xvi.
[2] Ibid., p. xvi [3] Ibid., p. xvii [4] Ibid., p xxxi [5] Ibid., p xxxii [6] Ibid., p xxxiii

THE POETICS OF THE HOUSE

Bachelard is not concerned with a description of the house, but instead, seeks to understand 'how we inhabit our vital space... how we take root, day after day in "a corner of the world." For our house is our corner of the world... a real cosmos in every sense of the word.' [1]

Bachelard sees the house as a shelter in a nurturing sense, not simply as shelter from the elements: 'Without it (the house) man would be a dispersed being. It maintains him through the storms of the heavens and through those of life. It is body and soul... Life begins well, it begins enclosed, protected, all warm in the bosom of the house.' [2]

Bachelard maintains that, in our subconscious, we see the house as a maternal entity and he quotes Rilke in support of his contention that 'the house holds childhood motionless "in its arms."' [2]

> '(House, patch of meadow, oh evening light
>   Suddenly you acquire an almost human face
>   You are near us, embracing and embraced.)' [3]

Bachelard sees the house as being rooted to the ground, a vertical entity with very different worlds in the cellar and the attic. The house stretches from the earth to the sky, a receptacle for daydreaming, this being enhanced if done in a tower. [4]

Constantly Bachelard explores those experiential meanings we experience in the various abodes within the house, movement having special significance. He describes how we become particularly aware of the way stairs lead <u>down</u> to the cellar but lead <u>up and down</u> to the bedchamber. [5]

[1] Bachelard, op.cit., p.4   [2] Ibid, p 7   [3] Ibid, p.8   [4] Ibid, p. 25   [5] Ibid, pp. 25, 26.

Bachelard makes connections between our experiences and our emotions, seeing experiences as extensions of ourselves. Stairs, windows, doors and rooms have a place in our deeper consciousness by virtue of their role in family life. To enter the house we must leave the outer world and cross the threshold to become part of the inner sanctum of the home. Because of this, the threshold has special significance.

In our homes 'the unconscious... is well and happily housed in the space of its happiness,'[1] but when man enters into life's adventures he must move outside the home. This movement is signified by the path, and Bachelard refers to George Sand's description: 'What is more beautiful than a road? It is the symbol and the image of an active and varied life!'[2]

Bachelard focuses on our attachment to familiar places of happiness, and on the way the home participates in our 'life of feelings'. The house enhances our experience of the storm or winter by its security and intimacy, becoming part of the 'drama that attaches to the dwellings of men.'[3]

The hearth receives special attention as the heart of the house. Bachelard uses writings by the novelist Bachelin to highlight Bachelin's relationship with his father: 'Comfortably seated in my chair I basked in the sensation of your strength.'[4] Bachelard sees this as belonging to 'the legendary images of primitive houses'.[5] For Bachelard, Bachelin:

> 'has only to give a few touches to the spectacle of the family sitting-room, only to listen to the stove roaring in the evening stillness, while an icy wind blows against the house, to know that at the house's center, in the circle of light shed by the lamp, he is living in the round house, the primitive hut, of prehistoric man'[6]

[1] Bachelard, op. cit., p. 10   [2] Ibid., p. 11   [3] A reference to the poet Rilke, Ibid., p 43   [4] Ibid., p. 31   [5] Ibid., p 31   [6] Ibid., p. 31

Bachelard identifies the sources of mankind's love for the house. Referring to his European experience, he explains how our feelings towards home become symbolized in images of rooms and stairs, fireplaces and furniture.

Roofs and chimneys symbolize shelter and warmth, windows become the 'eyes' of the house and recollections of winter strengthen the happiness of inhabiting.

In countries or regions where the idea of continuity has cultural significance, and where climatic and topographic conditions strongly influence the way of life, the preservation of traditional forms allows meaningful associations.

Britain is but one of many countries where there is a considerable and increasing demand for such associations, expressing desires that transcend issues of style, design or composition, because the symbolic meanings represented are central to existence.

Carter's Leaze, Great Walford, Warwickshire, England. New housing using tiles or slate roofing with dry stone walling and reclaimed materials such as old timber beams and stone floors. The houses are fitted with modern appliances, hand-built pine kitchens and carved stone fireplaces.

THE MIND OF THE UNIVERSE

Like Bachelard, the German philosopher Martin Heidegger (1889-1976) also believed that poetry could unlock fundamental truths about existence, truths that have become obscured by our twentieth century world-view. Poetry, not science, would reveal the essence of life to us because, as William Barrett has pointed out, poems, in Heidegger's view, elude 'the demands of our will.' [1] Barrett explains that 'The poet cannot will to write a poem, it just comes. And we as his readers cannot will our response either : we have to submit to the poem and let it work on us.'

Heidegger became convinced that twentieth century existence was characterized not only by man's domination of nature, but by his wilful exploitation of natural resources in an endless cycle of production and consumption. He believed that if we only see the world as a stockpile of raw materials for our gratification, we are missing the real point of existence.

Heidegger saw mankind as a unique form of consciousness and awareness through which the world is revealed. We are 'the vehicle for this perception; as Michael Zimmerman has described it, 'the mind of the universe'. [2] We are the 'clearing' through which the universe becomes conscious of itself.

Heidegger believed that instead of imposing our will on things, man should 'listen' and try to understand what the world really is. As Bryan Magee has pointed out 'if we really want to understand reality — we must try not to impose ourselves on it but rather submit ourselves to it.' [3] This thinking is similar to that of Buddhism or Hinduism, and to the world-view of the North American Indians, for whom the earth is sacred, not something to be owned or exploited.

[1] William Barrett in conversation with Bryan Magee, <u>Men of Ideas, Some Creators of Modern Philosophy</u>, BBC London, 1978, p87.   [2] Michael Zimmerman in a seminar conversation with the author at Tulane University.
[3] Bryan Magee, ibid., p. 87.

Heidegger felt that mankind had lost its 'cosmic roots' and that our production/exploitation mind set concealed from us our sense of belonging to a greater whole. He explained this whole as 'the fourfold,' seeing earth, sky, divinities and mortals as belonging together in what he describes as a 'mirroring play' where each is fully aware of the others.

Once, mankind had a sense of this interdependence, this belonging together. Daily life was intimately involved with the seasons and the passage of the sun and moon that give us day and night. As recently as medieval times, mankind relied on the seasons and the weather for his crops and needed the protection of the gods. Science and technology have dislocated us from our roots, from our participation in 'the fourfold,' so that we no longer live an authentic existence. This dislocation has not only obscured from us our role as guardians of the planet, but has also distorted our perception of the world we inhabit.

Heidegger makes his point that all things are interconnected, by using simple everyday objects, whose usage we take for granted. He uses a jug to illustrate how a scientific evaluation misses a whole dimension of experience. In so doing the jug becomes a metaphor for the world and our limited scientific perception of the world.

Heidegger argues that to the scientist a jug is a container in which, when filled, air is displaced by a fluid. But, as with other scientific descriptions, this misses the true role and nature of the jug. He points out that unlike inert objects such as a scythe or a hammer, the jug can nourish mankind in a significant manner, one that illuminates the belonging together of 'the fourfold.' He makes the distinction that pouring from a jug is not merely a functional act, but is, instead a gift. He explains the unseen origins of the jug's gift :

GIFTS

The jug may hold water. This comes from the spring, itself originating in the rock, 'and in the rock dwells the dark slumber of the earth, which receives the rain and dew of the sky'. For Heidegger, 'in the water of the spring dwells the marriage of sky and earth' and 'in the wine given by the fruit of the vine... the earth's nourishment and the sky's sun are betrothed to one another.' [1]

Heidegger's use of terms such as 'marriage' and 'betrothal' is significant. He sees earth and sky as joined in a loving relationship, one of mutual interdependence in which the one gives to the other: 'In the gift of water, in the gift of wine, sky and earth dwell.' [2] And when the wine is used at a religious service for consecration, 'The outpouring is the libation poured out for the immortal gods.'

Heidegger's message is that the way things belong to each other is more profound than their obvious, visible connection. It is a series of gifts that are concealed from us, instinctively felt by the poet, and he insists that 'the fourfold,' earth, sky, mortals and divinities dwell 'together all at once.' [3]

Seeing the cosmos in terms of supportive interaction, what John Ruskin called the 'law of help' present throughout nature, Heidegger extends the idea of 'the gift' to other things. A bridge, which seems merely to join, does more than that, it 'brings stream, bank and land into each other's neighbourhood. The bridge gathers the earth as landscape around the stream.' [4]

By stressing the gathering function of the bridge, Heidegger reinforces his main point, that the bridge, like the jug, is an instrument that enables things to belong to each other fruitfully. Like the jug, the bridge enriches our lives

[1] Martin Heidegger, Poetry, Language, Thought, Trans. by A. Hofstadter, New York, 1941, p. 172. [2] Ibid., p 172
[3] Ibid, p 173 [4] Ibid., p 152.

beyond its apparent function. Heidegger describes how city bridges lead from castle to cathedral, how in the countryside the bridge near the country town allows contact with surrounding villages. Always the bridge takes men to their various destinations.

Similarly, the Greek temple reveals the truth of man's belonging to 'the fourfold.' It rests on the earth, enhancing its situation, and in so doing 'first brings to light the light of the day, the breadth of the sky, the darkness of the night.'[1] Its repose 'brings out the raging of the sea.' It resists the storm and so 'makes the storm itself manifest in its violence.' The god is present in the temple, so like the jug and the bridge, the temple participates in a hidden network of supportive relationships.

The Greek temple reveals the way we are as part of 'the fourfold,' illuminating man's relationship to earth and sky, to the divinities, to light and darkness, to sun, moon and stars. According to Heidegger, the Greek temple authentically represents the life of a people, its values and its vocation.

For Heidegger, the artist would act as a kind of instrument to disclose things that transcend mankind's aims and interests. The work of art reveals to us what things already are but what we have been too blind to see. 'For genuine art to work it would have to reveal the fragility of human existence, its finitude and mortality.'[2]

Heidegger believed that for a true, mutually supportive and 'generous' interaction between man and nature, man should 'let things be' and the artist should enable things to show up as they are. He believed the poet had the greatest ability to reveal the true nature of things but he thought the architect should 'listen' to a site and should reveal its 'hidden' subtleties, so that our lives will be enhanced by a profound interaction between man and nature.

---

[1] Heidegger, Op. cit., p 42 [2] Michael E. Zimmerman, Heidegger's Confrontation with Modernity, Technology, Politics, Art, Bloomington, 1990, p 100

CONCLUDING SUMMARY

For thousands of years mankind evolved in a natural environment that was often hostile. In his struggle to survive he looked to the gods, seeking some control over those forces of nature on which he depended. Early cave drawings are sometimes seen as a means by which man could assert his dominance over nature, so art became a vehicle that helped him understand his world.

Above all, he sought security and protection, for which he looked to the gods. Amidst the uncertainty of the natural environment, man gained reassurance from order and permanence. Architecture could provide this, and for the ancient Egyptians, order, permanence and security were found in their temples and pyramids, each of which made connections with the gods and with nature. The pyramid is an artificial mountain that was a 'launching pad' to eternity, and in their temples, the Hypostyle Hall was an artificial forest that symbolized the way nature provided sustenance. The garden, throughout history, became another means of bringing nature under control. In all these endeavours, man is given a foothold in the world—he is no longer at its mercy—he gains a measure of control and understanding of natural forces.

The ancient Greeks understood the special qualities of sites believed to be inhabited by the gods. These sites were dedicated to the gods, who were personalized in order to humanize them. In this way they were brought within man's understanding. Man needed the support of the gods so he brought them into his world with buildings. Temples became a vital symbol of man's connection with the gods. They also represent those cultural values that distinguish the Greek civilization and on which the Western tradition was founded. By offering reassurance, security, and in providing cultural identity, the temple gave man an existential foothold on earth.

The Romans shifted the Greek preoccupation with the gods, nature and aesthetic sensitivity, towards order and control. Using the aesthetic system of the Greeks and providing temples in cities to house the gods, their urban architecture symbolized the power and organisational capacity of the Roman civilization. With the use of concrete in vaults, arches and domes, they developed structural systems that signified their intellectual prowess. With their propagandist architecture, roads, aqueducts and drainage systems, they provided early evidence of that cycle of control over nature and 'will to power' that, in Heidegger's view has led mankind to its present spiritual and experiential impoverishment.

Medieval architecture provided reassurance and hope in cathedrals that 'built' light to symbolize the divine.[1] Christianity conveyed the message of a personal god of love, compassion and forgiveness. The medieval town was fortified, enclosed, and with its cathedral, town hall and market square, it symbolized the idea of community, protection by the divine, and organization in the public realm.

In his seminal study, Genius Loci: Towards a Phenomenology of Architecture, Christian Norberg-Schulz, having carefully assimilated Heidegger's teachings, has incorporated Heidegger's main premises into a theoretical framework for the pursuit of architecture. Acknowledging Heidegger's postulation that the poet reveals the essence of the life-world, Norberg-Schulz argues that architecture 'represents a means to give man an "existential foothold"' in the world.[2]

He points out that man needs symbols in the form of works of art that represent 'life situations,' and that as man needs to experience his life as meaningful, the work of art (and architecture) enables him to keep and transmit meanings. Norberg-Schulz insists that for a meaningful life, man must comprehend his environment and must, therefore, bring it within terms of reference he can understand. He must be able to 'orientate

[1] C. Norberg-Schulz, Genius Loci: Towards a Phenomenology of Architecture, New York, 1980, p 56. [2] Ibid, p 5

TO DWELL POETICALLY ON EARTH

himself within and identify himself with an environment,' something that can only happen when life occurs in places that themselves have a strong sense of identity. [1]

He argues that the task of architecture is to clarify the true nature of the spirit of place, or as Heidegger might say 'to reveal the way man belongs to a particular place in terms of the earth, the sky and the divinities.'

In his perceptive and revelatory study, Norberg-Schulz addresses the way our feelings are affected by a world of 'people, of animals, of flowers, trees and forests, of stone, earth, wood and water, of towns, streets and houses, doors, windows and furniture, sun, moon and stars, of drifting clouds, of night and day and changing seasons' [2]

The significance of this will be understood by all who have spent time away from their homes or homeland. As Norberg-Schulz explains, our experience of our own city, region and country is unique, it is a particular and special experience of the world, of people, sport, humour, the media, of the sky, the breeze, the clouds and the seasons. Norberg-Schulz explains how we each grow to love our different habitats, whether we live in the tropics, a cold climate or a desert, and how this love is based on whether we are at home within a particular kind of landscape, with a particular mode of building or a particular way of life.

This philosophy refutes the notion of the 'global village' as a standardized entity, devoid of local character, as an inevitable path for mankind. This doomsday was predicted by Heidegger as he saw the threat of man's arrogant 'will to power.' He foresaw the consumer-driven despoliation of all that is unique, as man became increasingly insensitive to the way he belongs to the earth, the sky and the divinities. Norberg-Schulz is at pains to point towards the opposite, as he illuminates our understanding of the contribution that architecture can make to the way we may dwell authentically and poetically on earth.

[1] Norberg-Schulz, Op. cit, p. 5   [2] Ibid., p 6.

ANTOINE PREDOCK

In an interview with the author in 1993, Antoine Predock explained his approach to a house on the boardwalk at Venice beach, California:

'I thought the focus to the sea was a much more critical investigation than simply making a glass end wall... The foreground of the concrete before the sea is a black granite piece that is covered with a film of recirculating water. This glistening granite... connects... to the sea beyond, and there's a blurring then of sea, sky, water and polished granite. There's a yearning to the sea that begins to short circuit the imagined connection to the sea. I mean, this is the Venice boardwalk, there are bikes and roller skates and there's the beach and there's a lifeguard. Part of the mission of the house is to focus on those events...

The one ton pivot piece, the glazed pivot, that when open, allows the rush of the sea wind, the smell of the sea, the sound of the sea, to enter the house and is powder coated red, the colour of the Japanese flag. I was thinking of a morning in Japan near Ise on the shore. There I was in the land of the rising sun, watching it happen, thinking of the ritual importance of the sunrise in Japan. The homage in the colour of that window is to that culture... And there are other framing moves... terraces framing the view of sea and sky, isolating relationships between sea and sky or just sky...'.

House, Venice, California, Architect Antoine Predock. 1990

319